BERNARD SHAW ON THE PRESENT
STATE OF

THE CONTEMPORARY DRAMA
OF IRELAND

THE CONTEMPORARY DRAMA SERIES
Edited by Richard Burton

THE
CONTEMPORARY DRAMA
OF IRELAND

BY

ERNEST A. BOYD

BOSTON
LITTLE, BROWN, AND COMPANY
1917

Published February, 1917

Norwood Press
Set up and electrotyped by J. S. Cushing Co., Norwood, Mass., U.S.A.
Presswork by S. J. Parkhill & Co., Boston, Mass., U.S.A.

TO

H. L. MENCKEN

CONTENTS

THE CONTEMPORARY DRAMA
OF IRELAND

CHAPTER I

THE IRISH LITERARY THEATRE

THE last decade of the nineteenth century was
marked, in Germany, France, and England, by a
strong reaction against the decadence into which the
art of the theatre had fallen. When the *Freie Bühne*,
Théâtre Libre and Independent Theatre were established
their task was the by no means inconsiderable one of
driving from the stage the incredible sentimentalities
and the machine-made effects of the popular drama.
Most of the names which had for years occupied the
attention of playgoers are now lost in the obscurity
from which they should never have emerged. Occasionally touring companies are found, in the more un-
sophisticated regions, to galvanize the corpses of those
plays which excited the indignant ambition of the
progressive dramatists a quarter of a century ago.
Yet, in spite of undeniable progress, perhaps best
appreciated when the mid-Victorian play confers an

1

unmerited luster upon its modern Broadway equivalent, in spite of the advantages enjoyed by the successful play of to-day compared with its predecessors of the "eighties", it is generally admitted that the theatre badly responds to the intellectual demands of our time.

There is, however, one country whose drama shows a more than usual consistency in its intention to realize the ideals of the dramatic reformers who instituted the revolt against "Sardoodledom." Ireland did not escape the influences that were at work in Western Europe during the "eighteen-nineties" and which gave us, under Ibsen's impulse, a Hauptmann, a Brieux, and a Shaw. Instead, however, of springing up as an unrelated movement, in the midst of a universal acceptance of literary and dramatic commercialization, the Irish Dramatic Revival became at once a part of the comprehensive intellectual awakening which had then come to be known as "the Celtic Renaissance." Ever since 1880, when Standish O'Grady's epic history of Ireland had fired the imagination of a young generation of poets, Ireland had been giving forth unmistakable signs of the creative urge in national literature. W. B. Yeats and A. E. were already known to wide audiences, and the existence of a group of Irish poets and prose writers with a song and message refreshingly unlike the literature associated with *The Yellow Book* school, confirmed the truth of Ireland's Literary Revival. Consequently, when the wave of dramatic reform reached that country, just as the nineteenth century closed, it did not break against a stony indifference, nor was it diverted into shallow streams which soon dried up; it flowed naturally into the vital current of national literary activity.

The result has been that while the contemporaneous movements towards the reorganization of the theatre are now memories, with only here and there an isolated dramatist to testify to their passage, there is in Ireland to-day a national theatre, devoted, in the main, to the production of uncommercial drama. Without the State subvention necessary to the proper support of such an institution, the Irish Theatre has, for more than fifteen years, given practical effect to the plans and theories which inspired the "free stage" propagandists in Berlin, Paris, and London. The latter had to resign themselves to more temporary achievements, pending the time when their best talent might be absorbed by the theatre of commerce. The Irish Dramatic Movement has had to make concessions in order to obviate the difficulties arising out of economic dependence, but its evolution has been uninterruptedly in the direction of permanent success. It has not been supported by a coterie only but has enjoyed the satisfaction of seeing its public grow to meet its expansion, and above all, it has been creatively fruitful. That is to say, the Irish Theatre has not only educated the playgoer and influenced the dramatist, but has created a dramatic literature, and given birth to a number of playwrights whose genius would never have responded to any other call.

The association of the Irish drama with the Literary Revival is, therefore, so intimate that the limitations imposed upon the student are self-evident. He will concern himself neither with plays which accidentally or incidentally have their setting in Ireland, nor with the work of Irishmen whose spirit is as remote from their country as the scene in which their plays are laid.   Either of these conditions will exclude from consideration that excellent dramatization of Irish politics, *John Bull's Other Island*. On the other hand, the works of Oscar Wilde are, for obvious reasons, even more alien to the study of Irish drama than those of Calderon, who wrote *St. Patrick's Purgatory*, or of that sixteenth-century Italian dramatist, Giovanni Giraldi, whose *Arrenopia* found its scene in Limerick. Just as the non-Gaelic reader understands by Irish literature that body of prose and poetry which has been written during the past thirty years under the influence of the Celtic Renaissance, so he will apply the term Irish drama to the manifestation of that influence which has centered about the theatre.   There is an interesting Gaelic literature in the process of creation, and still more remarkable Gaelic drama, but neither calls for attention at the present time.   It will suffice to have recalled their existence, for they are the all important background in any attempt to picture the Anglo-Irish expression of our national life.

The almost immediate absorption of the "new drama" tendencies by the forces of the Literary Revival in Ireland must not, however, blind us to the fact that the Irish Theatre owes its birth to that general impulse of the period, and is not the purely "Celtic" creation generally supposed.   It was, at its inception, a local reaction to the prevalent stimulus, which impelled men to seek the renovation of an art abandoned to commercial speculation. The current misconception as to the origins and founders of our Dramatic Revival is due to the fame which accompanied the second phase of that revival, making of it the best known aspect of the Celtic Renaissance. We must, therefore, first establish the separate identity of the original Irish Literary Theatre, before coming to the now famous achievements of the Irish National Theatre Society. The former was essentially a part of the so-called "Ibsenite movement", which led to the establishment of the Independent Theatre in London; the latter was a part of the general renascence of Irish literature, whose progress made it possible for the national to embrace and transform the international movement of ideas.

Founded in 1899, the Irish Literary Theatre owed its title and, in a large measure its existence, to Edward Martyn, whose interest in the drama was avowedly stimulated by the revelation of Ibsen and the Scandinavian and Russian dramatists to a belated London public. With his friends George Moore and W. B. Yeats, of whom the former had contributed to the repertoire of the Independent Theatre, he projected his plan of giving Ireland a similar stage upon which literary plays might be performed, without being exposed to the exigencies of pure profiteering. His resolve was strengthened by the fact that he had been unable to find a London manager sufficiently appreciative to produce either *Maeve* or *The Heather Field*. These

composed his first volume of plays, which was published in 1899 and received most favorably by the
critics, thus emphasizing the necessity for a theatre
where such work could secure a hearing. Prior to
that date Martyn and Yeats had come over to Ireland
with a view to enlisting aid for their project. Lady
Gregory, A. E., Standish O'Grady, and a host of
others prominent in various departments of Irish life,
associated themselves with the proposal, and soon a
sufficient number of guarantors was found to bring
the Irish Literary Theatre into existence.

At the inaugural performance, which took place on
May 8, 1899, *The Countess Cathleen* by W. B. Yeats
occupied the program, and the following evening
Edward Martyn's *The Heather Field* was produced.
In February, 1900, a second season opened with *The
Bending of the Bough* by George Moore, which was
succeeded by Edward Martyn's *Maeve*, and a heroic
drama of ancient Ireland, *The Last Feast of the Fianna*,
by Alice Milligan, the sole contribution of importance
by this distinguished poetess to our dramatic literature. Finally, in October, 1901, the Irish Literary
Theatre terminated its official career, after the production of *Diarmuid and Grania*, written in collaboration by Yeats and Moore, and of the first Gaelic play
performed in any theatre, *Casadh an t-Sugáin* (The
Twisting of the Rope) by Douglas Hyde. In brief
summary, its achievement was the performance of six
plays in English, and one in Gaelic, all with Irish
themes, but played, with the exception of the last,
by English actors. It will be seen then, that while

an important step had been taken in the direction of a National Theatre, the essential condition of national drama, namely, native interpretation, was lacking.

It is doubtful, however, if the creation of a national drama was ever the main purpose of the enterprise. W. B. Yeats certainly had this object in view, but both his coadjutors were far more concerned to facilitate the production of literary drama, without special reference to its nationality. Consequently the plays produced reflect, as we shall see, this double tendency. Yeats, with the almost negligible support of Alice Milligan, represented the character which the Irish Theatre was subsequently to assume, whereas Martyn and Moore stood for the more cosmopolitan "drama of ideas" which they had learned to admire in London. The institution which they conceived would have given room to the poetic and folk plays of Yeats's ambition, but only on the same terms as would have been accorded to Chekhov or Strindberg. Elements of dissolution were contained in this clash of motives, so that the association of effort lasted only long enough to lay the foundation of the movement which was to give us a national theatre.

An examination of the work of Edward Martyn will enable us to estimate precisely the significance of his rôle in the evolution of contemporary Irish drama. It will then be evident why the Irish Literary Theatre must be traced to other sources than those from which the Irish National Theatre derives. At the same time, we shall notice the point of transition, which might have become one of fusion, had more foresight been

possible at the time. Martyn was not only the prime
mover of the Literary Theatre, but he most perfectly
embodies the dramatic ideal which that institution
represented, as against the aims subsequently formulated by the theory and practice of the Irish
National Theatre Society. While the plays of Yeats
and Alice Milligan contained no element irreconcilable
with the latter, those of Martyn have never become
part of the Irish Players' repertoire.

In order to appreciate the relation of theory to practice in Martyn's case, we must preface an analysis of
his writings by a brief exposition of the principles which
attended their production. These will be found in
Beltaine, which was, during the years 1899 and 1900,
"the organ of the Irish Literary Theatre." In the
first issue we read: "Everywhere critics and writers,
who wish for something better than the ordinary play
of commerce, turn to Norway for an example and an
inspiration." Then follows a reference to the *Théâtre
Libre* and Independent Theatre, and such inexpensive
theatres "which associations of men of letters hire
from time to time, that they may see on the stage the
plays of Henrik Ibsen, Maurice Maeterlinck, Gerard
Hauptmann, José Echegaray, or some less famous
dramatist who has written, in the only way literature
can be written, to express a dream which has taken
possession of his mind." The examples and influences
which prompted Martyn, Moore, and Yeats are evident from these opening lines of their manifesto, and,
that there should be no doubt as to their intentions,
they announce: "The Irish Literary Theatre will

attempt to do in Dublin something of what has been done in London and Paris;" adding, "if it has even a small welcome, it will produce, somewhere about the old festival of Beltaine, at the beginning of every spring, a play founded upon an Irish subject."

There is nothing in these statements which would expressly preclude the performance of the folk-plays and peasant drama now so completely identified with the Irish Theatre. Indeed, the editor of *Beltaine* seemed to have some such departure from the English and Continental models in his mind when he wrote: "The plays will differ from those produced by associations of men of letters in London and Paris, because times have changed, and because the intellect of Ireland is romantic and spiritual, rather than scientific and analytical." Nevertheless, it is impossible, when turning over the pages of *Beltaine*, to escape the feeling that the Scandinavian theatre, with its French and English disciples, was constantly in the minds of those who planned to give Ireland something analogous. Even the convention of the printed play, that essentially Shavian-English escape from the limitations of the commercial stage, was accepted. "In all or almost all cases the plays must be published before they are acted, and no play will be accepted which could not hope to succeed as a book." The popularity of the printed play has been largely due to the virtue which the "advanced dramatists" had to make of necessity, in the heroic days of the Ibsen-Shaw crusade. It has facilitated the de-dramatization of the contemporary "theatre of ideas", and does not deserve any more

respect than many another stage convention displaced
by the advent of the talking play — the "arguments",
"conversations", and other substitutes for drama in
recent years. Yet we find the Irish Literary Theatre
beginning its career with this conventional novelty of
the period, convinced apparently that some special
quality attaches to the work of a playwright who ad-
dresses himself to the reader first, to the playgoer afterwards.

Significantly, it will be found that the vast majority
of the plays in the repertoire of the National Theatre
make their appeal primarily to the eye and ear. They
appear in book form, it is true, but that is by no means
a condition precedent of their acceptance or success.
W. B. Yeats has written eloquently and at length
upon the claims of the poetic play, and of the relation
between "literature and the living voice", clearly
indicating a constant preoccupation far removed from
the interest of the printed plays as such. The speaking of verse has always been his chief concern in the
theatre, and the well-known superiority of the Irish
Players in their interpretation of poetic and peasant
plays is due to the rhythm of their speech. The English
actors, with the exception of Florence Farr, who played
during the three years of the Literary Theatre, could
not assert the superiority of the human voice over
print so wonderfully as the later group of players,
trained by the brothers Fay for the Irish National
Theatre. Consequently, this fact alone constituted a
serious obstacle to the reconcilement of the conflicting
ideals cherished by the founders of the original Theatre.

In the second number of *Beltaine* we find Yeats already confessing to a certain disappointment in his hope of having plays in verse adequately performed. After his experience with *The Countess Cathleen,* he writes: "I rather shrink from producing another verse play, unless I get some opportunity for experiment with my actors in the speaking of verse."

By way of summary we may say that the dominant note of *Beltaine* is cosmopolitan rather than national. While Yeats was pleading for dramas of Irish legend and classical history, his collaborators were arguing from the example of the dramatic innovations of Continental Europe. In support of the former there is little beyond vague announcements of plays, which have never materialized, by Fiona Macleod and Standish O'Grady; in support of the latter, there came articles dealing with the rise of the intellectual drama, and some of the most remarkable pieces written in English under the influence of Ibsen. On the one side was the theatre of beauty, on the other the theatre of ideas, concerned respectively for the importance of rhythm and diction and for the importance of the printed play. All the circumstances were propitious to the success of the latter, and unfavorable to the duration of an enterprise based upon so slight an identity of purpose. The only common ground was the general desire to follow an almost universal revolt against the stereotyped drama of the commercial theatre.

CHAPTER II

EDWARD MARTYN

GEORGE MOORE'S veracious essay in indiscreet autobiography, *Hail and Farewell,* contains no figure more interesting than Edward Martyn, who survives the ordeal of fictional reconstruction as successfully as A. E., and John Eglinton, in that all three emerge undiminished. Those three volumes of Irish literary history drew attention to the personality of many writers who would have preferred to let their own books speak for them, and Edward Martyn may be counted amongst their number. Biographically there is little to relate of him that bears upon his work for the Irish Theatre. A Nationalist of strong convictions, he has found himself involved in conflicts arising out of the clash of his political opinions with his social position as a landed gentleman and magistrate, in a country where these qualifications were traditionally dissociated from nationalism. He had long been a discriminating critic and lover of music, before the Dramatic Movement engaged his attention, a fact with which his country was made gratefully acquainted, when he donated fifty thousand dollars to found a Palestrina choir in the Catholic Pro-Cathedral, Dublin.

His artistic bent was not, however, solely in that direction which has provided the author of *Ave* with material for the exercise of a peculiar talent. When he left Dublin to complete his education at Oxford University, his fancy had turned to thoughts of poetry, and in 1885 he had prepared a book of verse for publication, but in spite of his twenty-six years and his Irish birth, he resisted the impulse, and destroyed the manuscript. It was not until 1890 that he made his first venture into literature, when he published *Morgante the Lesser*, under the pseudonym, "Sirius." This extraordinary novel did not reveal anything of the future dramatist. It was a brutal satire, Swiftian in its manner, upon the scientifico-materialistic philosophy of that period when the omnipotence of Darwinian rationalism had not yet been rationally disputed. Written in the elaborate, discursive fashion of the eighteenth-century satirists, the book was not one to appeal to the average novel reader, but it deserves attention, if only because of a reflected interest which his subsequent works have conferred upon it. We shall see that his conception of the nature of satire did not materially alter when he came to project his fancies upon the stage.

In 1899 he published *The Heather Field* and *Maeve* in one volume, with a preface by George Moore, and these were the two plays which constituted the greatest successes of the Irish Literary Theatre, where they were almost immediately produced. So successful was *The Heather Field* that it was performed shortly afterwards in London and New York, and was translated for production in Germany. In confirmation of what has

already been said as to the examples by which the
founders of the Irish Literary Theatre were inspired,
we find in George Moore's preface a characteristic
analysis of the Independent Theatre movement in
London. With considerable irony he describes his
adventures with Mr. William Archer, the champion of
Ibsen, and with the managers or actors who professed
to be interested in literary drama. As he rightly says,
the collapse of the theatre of ideas in London was
mainly due to the indiscriminate enthusiasm of the
critics, and the public led by them, for all plays which
seemed in any way to depart from the conventional
success of the Sardou-Rostand type. Pinero, in particular, is accused by Moore of having utterly demoralized
the advocates of progress, who mistook his suburban
audacities for advanced ideas, and his literary melodrama for a new technique. Incidentally, it transpires that neither the producers nor the critics could
be induced by Moore to consider favorably *The Heather
Field*. Obviously, we must conclude that Martyn's
aim was to write for the existing London theatres open
to literary plays, and not to found a theatre for the
special purpose. Finding no encouragement he then
bethought himself of a joint undertaking, with Yeats
and Moore as his active supporters, — the former
having experienced London production, when his
Land of Heart's Desire was played at the Avenue
Theatre in 1894, the latter having shared in the work
of the Independent Theatre, where *The Strike at Arling-
ford* was produced in 1893.

The three acts of *The Heather Field* are devoted to

a psychological analysis of Carden Tyrrell, the Irish landowner, whose world of reality is situated in the land of his own dreams, but who has been forced to grapple with the material factors of life in the administration of his estate. Although marriage has thrust the duties and responsibilities of his position upon him, Tyrrell is temperamentally incapable of abandoning himself wholly to everyday affairs. The idealist in him soon conceived the quixotic passion of reclaiming from the Atlantic a wild field of bog and heather, and when the play opens we find him immersed in the plans and difficulties attendant upon the realization of his dream. He has mortgaged his property heavily to obtain money for the work of draining and removing the rocks from the heather field, and his wife is anxious to secure control of the estate, in order to prevent him from utterly ruining their fortunes, by raising further loans to repair the damage caused to the adjoining land, in the course of improving the field in question. Tyrrell has allowed his passion so to possess him that he has become oblivious to everything, and clings with increasing desperation to what he feels is his lost ideal. He is in a state of intense exaltation, aggravated by the constant antagonism of a very matter-of-fact wife, whose sympathy for him was never deep, and is now turned to a mixture of fear and hatred, by the spectacle of the inevitable bankruptcy into which they are drifting.

The strangeness of her husband's manner, his visionary intensity, and the obvious calamity which threatens to engulf her and their child, serve to provide Mrs.

Tyrrell with the weapon she requires. In the typical Strindbergian manner she sets herself to have her husband declared incompetent on the ground of insanity. The alienists are on the point of giving the verdict which will place the direction of Tyrell's affairs in his wife's hands, but are dissuaded by his close friend, Barry Ussher. The latter, knowing and loving Tyrrell, cannot accept the theory of madness, and although he appreciates the difficulty of Mrs. Tyrrell's position, he cannot permit an action whose effect would assuredly be to drive the idealist insane. Tyrrell is thus saved from being put under restraint, but the catastrophe feared by Ussher is merely postponed. His mortgages and debts have transformed the erstwhile lenient landlord into a hard taskmaster, who turns to eviction, as did so many of his fellows, as the way out of his own incapacity and bad management. The evicted tenants have resorted to the violence which was long the only expression of their side of the agrarian campaign in Ireland, and Tyrrell has been provided with a police escort to protect him from the vengeance of his tenantry. This protection is so repulsive to him that he prefers to remain indoors, brooding over his dream, and slipping farther away from contact with the present.

As he lives at home, thrown back upon himself and cherishing memories as a refuge from his unhappy present, Carden Tyrrell becomes ever more engrossed in the symbolic vision of the heather field, where the winds sang to him of youth and happiness, whose flowering represents the consummation of joy and success. But one day his little child comes to him with a handful of heather buds, the only flowers he could find while playing in that field of fate. These announce the triumph of nature over Tyrrell's efforts; the land he would reclaim has become waste once more, so that not even this ideal world is left in which he could wander in fancy. The blow destroys his dream and his reason, but only for a moment. In ecstatic vision he reasserts his idealism, for he has crossed forever the line which divides the material from the imaginative, and the curtain falls upon the man restored at last to the period of his youth, when the earth was fair and his spirit untroubled.

The part of Ibsen in the conception of *The Heather Field* seems perhaps more obvious than it really is. The *leitmotiv* derives something from *The Wild Duck*, and there is more than a suggestion of *Ghosts* in the closing scene, when Tyrrell turns to his child, whom he believes to be his brother and cries: "See, even now the sky is darkening as in that storm scene of the old legend I told you on the Rhine. See, the rain across a saffron sun trembles like gold harp strings, through the purple Irish Spring!" And then, as they watch the rainbow: "Oh, mystic highway of man's speechless longings! my heart goes forth upon the rainbow to that horizon of joy!" (*With fearful exaltation.*) "The voices — I hear them now triumphant in a silver glory of song."

George Moore asserts that it was "the first play written in English inspired by the examples of Ibsen", a fact of which he failed to convince Mr. Archer, who held, of course, that the great Scandinavian dramatist was essentially a social reformer. In that sense it is impossible to describe Edward Martyn as "an Irish Ibsen", for he has never professed any didactic intention, and it would be hard to say wherein consists the "purpose" of *The Heather Field*. As Moore pointed out, we sympathized with Tyrrell, "although all right and good sense are on the wife's side." This, however, was not the case in London, where, we have the authority of Yeats for saying, the audience approved of the proposal to lock up Tyrrell as a madman. In Ireland the doctors were hissed by the less sophisticated members of the audience, as a sign of their disapproval of Mrs. Tyrrell's intentions! The fact is, as further examination will prove, the work of Martyn may be described as essentially Ibsenite, or not, — according as one emphasizes the propagandist aspect of Ibsen's dramas. Inasmuch as the latter has been the point upon which his English disciples have insisted, their plays have all tended to become vehicles for the expression of social theories. As the Irish playwright avoided this procedure he cannot be termed a follower of Ibsen, as the expression is usually employed.

Naturally, Edward Martyn was subjected to the Norwegian influence, and so far as the latter has colored modern dramatic technique, he is truly a product of the period. He seems, nevertheless, to have given a more personal imprint to his rendering of the lesson learned by his contemporaries from Ibsen. Instead of merely seizing upon the facilities for propaganda afforded by the abolition of worn-out conventions, he applied Ibsen's method to the portrayal of national character and the interpretation of Irish life. Consequently, his plays resemble those of his master much more than does anything written by the author of the *Quintessence of Ibsenism*, who has been so instrumental in obscuring the true purpose of the dramatist. While Shaw has read into Ibsen a most interesting commentary upon contemporary social problems, he has caused us to lose sight of the original spirit in which that commentary was presented. There have been innumerable minor variations upon such themes as *The Doll's House*, but none of the later English playwrights has approached a local theme in the Ibsen manner. In Martyn we get the essence of Ibsenism, rather than that quintessence extracted by Bernard Shaw. He does not concentrate upon one aspect of Ibsen's genius, but envelops his subject in an atmosphere which we recognize as akin to that of *Hedda Gabler* or *The Lady from the Sea*.

A notable example of this adaptation is *Maeve*, the "psychological drama in two acts", which followed *The Heather Field* in the published volume, as also on the stage of The Irish Literary Theatre. Maeve O'Heynes, daughter of The O'Heynes, hereditary Prince of Burren, County Clare, is an idealist of the same visionary race as Carden Tyrrell. She has submitted to betrothal with a wealthy Englishman, Hugh FitzWalter, from a sense of duty to the impoverished nobility of her father, who cannot occupy the rank to which he is entitled without the fortune which this marriage will bring. From the moment the curtain

is raised, Maeve is revealed as a dreamy, high-strung
girl, whose imagination is haunted by the fairy lore
and legend of the countryside. She moves on a plane
of vision far above the humdrum world of her impecu-
nious family, whose sole thought is the marriage which
will restore their social dignity. Maeve has nothing
in common with her young English suitor, who shows
himself, indeed, strangely tolerant of the indifference,
amounting to aversion, with which she meets his
expressions of sentiment. It is understood, however,
that the girl is more than usually sensitive and moody,
and much latitude is granted her in the expression of
her temperament.

The confidant of Maeve's dreams is the old nurse,
Peg Inerny, who has all the West Irish peasant's
poetic faith in the existence of "the good people",
the superhuman beings of the Celtic land of faery.
Peg is convinced that the lore of the peasantry identi-
fying her with the Great Queen Maeve of Gaelic epic
history is based upon the fact that she undergoes this
metamorphosis at night upon the mountain side.
She finds in Maeve O'Heynes one only too ready to
follow her into this existence of the spirit, for Peg
speaks to the visionary girl of things seen in moments
of rapture. Thus, when the old nurse invites her out
on to the mountain to meet the great figures of legend,
and the noble lover revealed in her dreams, Maeve
forgets her wedding eve and accompanies her. After
several hours of trance on the hills, she returns to the
old castle, her whole being disturbed by the ecstasy
of vision. She seats herself at the open window, in-

sensible of the piercing cold of the night, and as she broods, the spirit world opens to her, and before her eyes there passes the procession of Queen Maeve with her attendants, as they rise out of the mountain cairn and come towards the castle. On their return they are accompanied by the spirit of Maeve, which passes with the others into the mysterious realm of Tir-nan-ogue. When her sister comes to prepare her for the wedding she finds the bride sitting cold and lifeless at the window, her soul having gone out to meet that of the ideal lover — himself but a symbol of eternal beauty.

Both W. B. Yeats and George Moore have seen in *Maeve*, to quote the latter, "the spirit and sense of an ill-fated race." "She portrays its destiny and bears the still unextinguished light of its heroic period." Or as the editor of *Beltaine* expressed it, the play was a symbol of "Ireland's choice between English material-ism and her own natural idealism, as well as the choice of every individual soul." In a remarkable essay Yeats has discussed " Maeve and Certain Irish Beliefs", in which he illustrates the background of experience from which such characterizations as that of Peg Inerny take their reality. Edward Martyn did not profess to have drawn this character from life, but, as Yeats shows, the peasant belief in women who are queens "when in faery" is widespread. As a footnote to the folklore of the play this essay from *Beltaine* is worth preserving. But, without any reference to such inquiries, *Maeve* is a noteworthy contribution to our dramatic literature. Spectacularly it is most effective, more especially in the scene where the vision of Queen Maeve comes to the young girl in her trance, a fitting climax to the cold, unearthly movement of the entire play, whose atmosphere is finely conceived and sustained.

In 1902 appeared a second volume of plays containing *The Tale of a town* and *The Enchanted Sea*. The former was written for the second season of the Irish Literary Theatre, but was not produced in its published form. Instead of the latter was substituted *The Bending of the Bough*, a rewritten version by George Moore which appeared in book form in 1900, shortly after its production. Nothing in the preface indicated that the play was any other but Moore's invention, and it was not until the following year that he explained how he had revised *The Tale of a Town*:

"In my re-writing . . . the two plays have very little in common except the names of the personages and the number of the acts. The Comedy, entitled *The Bending of the Bough*, was written in two months, and two months are really not sufficient time to write a five act comedy in; and, at Mr. Martyn's request, my name alone was put on the title page."

Since these lines were written in the 1901 issue of *Samhain* (the successor of *Beltaine* as the organ of the Dramatic Movement), readers of *Hail and Farewell* have been fully initiated into the circumstances of the transfer of authorship. It says a great deal for Edward Martyn's enthusiasm for the Irish Literary Theatre that he should have effaced himself to the extent of handing over his play to another.

It is a little difficult nowadays, when one reads the two versions, to understand why *The Tale of a Town* should have been rejected in favor of *The Bending of the Bough*, which has not added anything to the reputation of George Moore. Both plays are substantially the same, although four out of the five acts were rewritten in *The Bending of the Bough*. The action centers about the struggle of Jasper Dean, alderman of a coast town in the west of Ireland, to unite the members of the corporation in the defense of their municipal rights. The town is owed an indemnity by the municipality of Anglebury, an English watering place, whose line of steamers has secured the elimination of competition by promising to pay the Irish line compensation for the latter's retirement from business. Various social and political jealousies and influences have prevented the aldermen from effectively joining to enforce their lawful demands upon the city council of Anglebury. The author exposes in the crudest and most brutal fashion the sordid intrigues of municipal politics, showing how the interests of the public are sacrificed to the play of personal motives. Jasper Dean, however, is a patriot, and a man of caliber and intelligence, who eventually succeeds in dominating the situation. His obvious disinterestedness enables him to unite the whole council, with the exception of one opportunist, and it looks as if the Irish town were at last on the point of securing its rights. In the end Dean is corrupted by the influence of his intended wife, who is the niece of the mayor of Anglebury. Very subtly she is used to poison his mind with the sophistries

which have ever appealed to the anti-patriotism of a
certain class of Irishmen. The social advantages of preferring England to Ireland are once again demonstrated,
and once again this appeal to class prejudice succeeds.
᠄ The difference between the two plays is one of manner, not of matter, for in both cases the conclusion is
the same. Moore had the advantage of his craftsman-
ship as novelist to help him over the places where
Martyn stumbled, but it is doubtful if his play reflects
adequately the disparity of literary stature between
the two authors. In spite of that youthful effort in
tragedy, *Martin Luther* (1879), and notwithstanding
the marked improvement between *The Strike at Arling-
ford* (1893) and *The Apostle* (1911), *Esther Waters*
(1913), and *Elizabeth Cooper* (1913), George Moore
does not possess the gift of writing for the stage. His
technique will not permit him to secure in the theatre
those effects which are so great a charm of his fiction,
autobiographical or otherwise. Consequently, while
he has softened the harsh caricature of Martyn's
picture of municipal politics, and made more universally
intelligible the desertion of Jasper Dean, he has not
made *The Bending of the Bough* a great play. In fact,
for all its crudity, *The Tale of a Town* is more faithful
in its interpretation of Irish conditions. So little did
the latter concern Moore that he transported the
setting to Scotland, thus ignoring the essential part of
Martyn's satire. For the fundamental interest of the
play as originally conceived is its symbolical interpretation of Irish political conditions, to which is
added, of course, the satire of actual city politics.

When *The Tale of a Town* was eventually performed in
Dublin, in 1905, this aspect of the play at once caught
attention and made it a success. *The Bending of the
Bough* might stand as the type of political comedy in
general, *The Tale of a Town* representing Irish political
comedy in particular. The precise significance of
Jasper Dean's betrayal is more intelligible to Ireland
in Martyn's version than in Moore's, but in the latter
it will be more easily understood by a public unfamiliar
with local circumstances. For this reason foreign
commentators have invariably preferred *The Bending
of the Bough;* which is possibly a better written play,
but is not, therefor, a better Irish play.

In *The Enchanted Sea*, the author returned to a theme
more akin to his talent than political satire, which he
again essayed, however, in 1902, when *The Place
Hunters* was published in an Irish review, *The Leader.*
This trifle is sufficiently indicated by its title and need
not detain us. *The Enchanted Sea*, on the other hand,
must be bracketed with *Maeve*, as an interesting application of Ibsen's method to the material of Irish
life. More than any other work of Martyn's, this
play bears the mark of the Scandinavian dramatist's
influence, being, in fact, an Irish counterpart to *The
Lady from the Sea.* Guy Font, like Ibsen's heroine,
has been glamoured by the call of the sea. Living
among the peasantry on the wild Atlantic seaboard of
Ireland's west coast, the boy had imbibed their legends
of the element by which he is fascinated. His strange,
impractical disposition makes him an easy prey to the
designs of his aunt, Mrs. Font, who has been deprived

of her late husband's estates by the death of their son. The Font property has passed to her nephew Guy, to the intense chagrin of Mrs. Font, who had schemed and plotted during her husband's lifetime to advance their welfare at the expense of his honor. This erratic lad, heedless of everything but the voice of the sea, stands between her and her purpose of possession, and her one desire is to remove him.

Mrs. Font, could she encompass the death of Guy, would be able, she fancies, to realize a double purpose. Once she had secured the estates they would serve as sufficient dowry to attract Lord Mask into marrying her daughter, Agnes. Mask is the only friend of Guy in all this circle of commonplace or scheming individuals, for despite the difference in their ages, these two are united by the common fascination exercised upon them by the sea and its mystery. Mrs. Font decides to put this fascination to account in so far as it affects the boy, by hearkening to that peasant instinct in herself which hints that Guy Font is one of the sea fairies. She persuades him to show her a cave where he is in the habit of communing with the spirits of the sea, and they depart together. When she returns alone, some time later, suspicion falls upon her, but not before she has been disappointed of her last hope. Lord Mask, unbalanced by the death of his young friend, seeks to find Guy in the waves, which finally carry him off to join the young lad in another world. When the police come to arrest Mrs. Font, they find her hanging dead from the staircase of Fonthill, where she has used the child's swing to commit suicide.

When *The Enchanted Sea* was performed at the
Ancient Concert Rooms, Dublin, in 1904, — the scene
of the inauguration of the Dramatic Revival, — it was
received with much attention, in spite of the inadequate
interpretation it then was given. As published, it is
marred by clumsiness of characterization which might
easily be concealed by the performance of a good company. The characters are finely conceived and if
presented by capable actors they would certainly lose
something of the stiffness which renders them artificial
or lifeless in the printed play. On the whole, it must
be said that Edward Martyn has done very well by a
theme which, in the nature of things, could be saved
from melodrama only by the hand of a master dramatist.

A long interval separates these two volumes of plays
from the next work for the theatre which Edward
Martyn was to issue in book form. When the three
experimental years of the Irish Literary Theatre expired, and the partnership of Yeats, Moore, and Martyn
was dissolved, the last-mentioned writer found himself
isolated in a literary community whose main interest
was in the direction of folk-drama. He had, therefore,
but little incentive to write, being dependent for the
performance of his work upon amateur organizations,
such as The Players Club, which produced *An Enchanted Sea*, and The National Players, who were
responsible for *The Tale of a Town*. It was not until
these spasmodic and unrelated forces, working for the
advancement of intellectual drama, had crystallized
into a more permanent form, that Martyn's creative

activities were aroused. During many years he was a supporter of every kind of theatrical enterprise which promised to make Ireland acquainted with the better class drama of our time, an experience which we could not expect to enjoy at the hands of our Anglicized theatres of commerce. At last, The Independent Theatre Company promised to become an institution of the kind associated with the name of its English prototype of twenty years ago.

This association undertook to produce literary plays, irrespective of the national character, and one of its earliest performances was that of Edward Martyn's *Grangecolman* in 1912. Although it came so long after the author's previous work, this play showed in him the same preoccupation with the psychological drama as in the days of Ibsenism. *Rosmersholm* was suggested to several critics by this narrative of a daughter's jealousy, when she finds herself supplanted in the life of her father by the secretary whom he purposes to marry. Catharine Devlin is a typical product of the feminist movement, as it is revealing itself in the first moments of discontent and disillusionment. In order to escape the duties of her home, she introduces Clare Farquhar to act in her stead as amanuensis to her father, but she returns to find that he and Clare have found happiness in the reciprocal help of their relationship. While Catharine and her ineffective husband drift aimlessly along, cherishing barren ideals, they form a striking contrast to the quiet industrious contentment of the home which she once fled as a burden. Having failed in her career as a doctor, and disappointed

in her demands upon life, Catharine is stirred, like
another Hedda Gabler, by the spectacle of her father's
dependence on, and trust in, Clare Farquhar. She
must, at all costs, destroy the happiness which she
herself has never known. Grangecolman is haunted
by a family ghost, and she conceives the idea of impersonating this phantom for the purpose of frightening
Michael Colman and Clare. But the latter is unim-
pressed by the bogey, in spite of the evident fears of
the other members of the household, and when the
white-robed figure makes its appearance, a revolver
shot ends the fable and, at the same time, the existence
of Catharine Devlin.

The faulty characterization and a certain amateurish-
ness, noticeable in the earlier plays, are almost wholly
absent from *Grangecolman*, which shows that the
intervening years have left their experience of the stage
upon Edward Martyn. The mystic, symbolic Ibsenism of *Maeve* and *The Heather Field* has made way for
a cold realism, which holds the spectator by the intensity of its reflection of reality. The characteristic
touch of Scandinavian melodrama is not wanting, but
the author is able to carry it off as successfully as did
Ibsen before him. When one sees how Martyn has
triumphed over his natural tendency towards an over-
formal dialogue, one cannot but regret that his talent
should have lain almost quiescent for want of an occasion for its exercise. He has had to content himself with
amateur performances, where the defects inevitable in
such associations have done little to render supple his
dramatic speech. He has never enjoyed the inestimable

good fortune which befell the successors of the Irish
Literary Theatre. They found interpreters who were
not only born to fit their parts, but whose histrionic
powers have saved from oblivion many a play of no
greater intrinsic merit than those of Edward Martyn.

Early in 1915, the reward of many years of waiting
and patient effort came to the founder of the Irish
Literary Theatre, when his original plan was resusci-
tated, this time under the title, "The Irish Theatre."
A satirical comedy by Edward Martyn, *The Dream
Physician*, and two new works by young Irish playwrights were produced, in the course of the first two
seasons, in addition to plays by Chekhov. To complete the illusion of former days, George Moore was
among the spectators at one of the *premières*, a fact
which he signalled in a letter to the press, announcing
the resumption of his interrupted relations with Edward
Martyn, and repeating the original terms of his dramatic creed. Clearly a case of history repeating itself.
Yet, not quite, for there is every reason to suppose
that this renewal of effort will not have the brief career
of what was, after all, a mere experiment. There is
felt to be an increasing need for a theatre in Ireland
which will hold up to nature that half of the mirror
which is not visible in the Irish National Theatre,
where a too exclusive care for the folk drama has resulted in giving a one-sided appearance to our dramatic
activities. This is precisely the rock upon which the
first movement split, as we shall see in the next chapter.
Meanwhile, it is satisfactory to note that the stand
taken by Edward Martyn, nearly twenty years ago,

has at last been translated into practical terms, by the creation of a theatre to carry on the work he has disinterestedly served in the face of much discouragement. Not the least of his disadvantages has been the phenomenal popularity of an enterprise representing the very opposite tendency to that which he championed from the beginning.

CHAPTER III

The Beginnings of the Irish National Theatre

In the first number of *Samhain* (1901–1908), which was destined to be the organ of the Irish National, as distinct from the Irish Literary, Theatre, W. B. Yeats wrote the epitaph of the initial experiment. "Whether the Irish Literary Theatre has a successor made on its own model or not, we can claim that a dramatic movement, which will not die, has been started." And that is, indeed, the principal achievement of those three years which ended as the words were written. Of the plays performed, only those of Edward Martyn were in themselves important, excepting, of course, *The Countess Cathleen*, which belongs more properly to the second phase of the Dramatic Revival. The *Diarmuid and Grania* of Moore and Yeats was not any better than so unusual a collaboration would lead one to anticipate, but it shared the program of the final season with Douglas Hyde's *The Twisting of the Rope*, whose performance was productive of much good. In the first place it gave the impulse to a whole school of Gaelic dramatists, and in the second, it drew attention to the superiority and desirability of Irish actors,

having been performed by native players, unlike all
the other plays of the Irish Literary Theatre, which
were produced by English companies.

The actors in this Gaelic production were amateurs,
trained by W. G. Fay, who had previously organized
the Ormond Dramatic Society. His work with this
Society made him realize the possibility that lay in
the extension to Anglo-Irish plays of the advantages
of native interpretation enjoyed by the Gaelic, and
when his brother Frank read the first act of A. E.'s
Deirdre in *The All Ireland Review*, they decided to make
this play the starting point of their experiment.   A. E.
completed his poetic drama of Irish legend, rehearsing
in a small hall, in emulation of Antoine of the *Théâtre
Libre* and not content with that, he interested Yeats
in the group.   Soon the latter's *Cathleen ni Houlihan*
was added to their new repertoire, and both plays were
produced in April, 1902.   The following October, in
the second issue of *Samhain*, the Fays' Irish National
Dramatic Company was formally recognized as the
legitimate successor of the Irish Literary Theatre, and
the second phase of the Dramatic Movement was
definitely inaugurated.   As emphasizing the separate
and independent origin of the existing National Theatre,
W. B. Yeats's announcement in *Samhain* may be
quoted: "The Irish Literary Theatre has given place
to a company of Irish actors.   Its Committee saw them
take up the work all the more gladly because it had not
formed them or influenced them."   And a little further
on we find him enthusiastic in praise of the acting:
"It was the first performance I had seen, since I under-

stood these things, in which the actors kept still enough to give poetical writing its full effect upon the stage. I had imagined such acting, though I had not seen it."

These quotations sufficiently indicate to what extent the tradition of acting which gave its strength to the Irish Players, and conferred distinction upon the Irish National Theatre, was due to forces entirely different from those which lay behind the first manifestation of the Dramatic Revival. By the time the latter was nearing its close, there had come into existence an association which corresponded far more closely to the ideal which Yeats had in view. Once A. E. had brought him into contact with the brothers Fay and their enterprise, there could be no longer any doubt as to which branch of dramatic activity he would favor. Martyn, on the other hand, did not share his enthusiasm, so there could be no question of his following Yeats. In due course Yeats was elected president, and A. E. vice president, of the Irish National Dramatic Society. Lady Gregory and others rallied to this new association, and it became certain that the Irish Theatre was definitely committed to a program somewhat unlike that conceived by Martyn and Moore. The former did not abandon hope immediately, but proceeded to criticize his colleagues for their shortsighted support of an undertaking utterly different from their own Literary Theatre. In reply to this criticism, and in explanation of the true intentions of the Movement, Yeats delivered himself as follows:

Mr. Martyn argued in *The United Irishman* some months ago that our actors should try to train themselves for the modern drama of society. The acting of plays of heroic life, or plays like *Cathleen ni Houlihan*, with its speech of the country people, did not seem to him a preparation. It is not; but that is as it should be. Our movement is a return to the people. . . . and the drama of society would but magnify a condition of life which the countryman and the artisan could but copy to their hurt. The play that is to give them a quite natural pleasure should either tell them of their own life, or of that life of poetry where every man can see his own image, because there alone does human nature escape from arbitrary conditions. Plays about drawing-rooms are written for the middle classes of great cities, for the classes who live in drawing-rooms, but if you would uplift the man of the roads you must write about the roads, or about the people of romance, or about great historical people.

This quotation, which amounts to a confession of literary faith, appeared in the same 1902 issue of *Samhain* that proclaimed the Fays and their company the rightful successors of the Irish Literary Theatre. Nothing could more clearly establish the point at issue between the two, or more unequivocally declare the complete identity of Yeats's ideals with those of the brothers Fay, whom he admitted, as we have seen, to have formed independently their conclusions as to what should constitute the work of an Irish National Theatre. Although Yeats himself has placed on record the priority of the Fays' claim, that fact is not usually insisted upon in popular accounts of the Dramatic Movement in Ireland. It is, however, important, not only as a matter of historical justice, but also because its avoidance has resulted in a tendency to overlook the presence in that movement of two phases, — the one international and initiated by Martyn, Yeats, and Moore under the force of continental European example, the other intensely national, and due to the work of two men of histrionic genius, aided by a group of young poets and dramatists.

This circle included several names subsequently to become well known to lovers of Anglo-Irish literature, such as Padraic Colum, Seumas O'Sullivan and James Cousins. To these may be added J. M. Synge, although he did not come into the movement until later, in 1903, when the control of the Fays' enterprise had passed into the hands of W. B. Yeats and Lady Gregory. Prior to that event, the Irish National Dramatic Company had made itself responsible for the production of some half-dozen plays, of which the following were afterwards published in book form: *Deirdre* by A. E., *Cathleen ni Houlihan* by W. B. Yeats, *The Sleep of the King* by James Cousins, and *A Pot of Broth* by W. B. Yeats. In the order mentioned, they occupied the program of the Society during its two seasons of 1902. In the early part of the following year a prospectus was issued stating that: "The Irish National Theatre Society was formed to continue on a more permanent basis the work of the Irish Literary Theatre." In a sense this statement is correct, inasmuch as W. G. Fay's Irish National Dramatic Company had been recognized in *Samhain* as the successor of the Literary Theatre. But, as we have seen, his Company was already in existence, independently of the undertaking of Martyn and Yeats. It would, therefore, be more accurate to say that the Irish National Theatre Society was formed to carry on the work which the Fays had initiated, as, indeed, the slight variation of title itself implies.

The year 1903 saw the arrival of J. M. Synge, and the active participation of Lady Gregory in the movement which she had heretofore supported in a less prominent fashion. The latter's *Twenty-Five* and the former's *In the Shadow of the Glen,* together with Padraic Colum's *Broken Soil,* introduced for the first time three dramatists who have since contributed to the Irish Theatre its most characteristic and most remarkable work. As if to emphasize the distinction of a year marked by the revelation of these talents, and further enriched by the production of two of Yeats's most beautiful plays, *The Hour Glass* and *The King's Threshold,* 1903 is also the date of America's entrance into the history of the Theatre. The then recently founded Irish Literary Society of New York produced *The Pot of Broth* and *Cathleen ni Houlihan,* in addition to Yeats's *Land of Heart's Desire,* which had been revived in this country in 1901, after its original production at the Avenue Theatre, London, in 1894, but curiously enough, was not performed in Dublin until ten years later. Finally, the year witnessed the first tour abroad of the Irish Players, who went to London and performed five pieces from their current repertoire to a select but enthusiastic audience. The result of that visit was to bring the Dramatic Revival to a turning point in its evolution, with consequences whose end is not yet in sight.

An Englishwoman, Miss A. E. F. Horniman, who had for many years devoted herself to the support of the repertory theatre, was so deeply impressed by the qualities of the Irish Players and their plays, that she resolved to give substantial form to her approval. Heretofore they had been obliged to perform in concert halls and similar places, wholly devoid of the scenic and seating accommodation suitable for theatrical performances. Miss Horniman obtained the lease of the Mechanics' Institute, Dublin, a small theatre which had been given over to vaudeville of the roughest kind. She enlarged and rebuilt it, and, under the name of the Abbey Theatre, it became the home of the Irish Players, rent free, for a period of six years, from 1904. During that time a small annual subsidy was also part of Miss Horniman's gift, but in 1910 this was withdrawn, when the Abbey Theatre was purchased from her by public subscription.

The absence of a subsidy, and the financial obligations involved in this purchase, were to have their effect upon the fortunes of the Irish Theatre, but there can be little doubt as to the value of the services rendered by Miss Horniman during the *Sturm und Drang* period of its existence. The economic independence which made possible the resistance subsequently offered to the exigencies of ignorance was solely due to her magnanimity in giving Ireland " the first endowed Theatre in any English-speaking country", as Yeats described it. It was not until 1907 that Miss Horniman conferred a similar advantage upon her own country by establishing in Manchester the now famous

Gaiety Theatre, as the first repertory theatre in Great Britain. This institution has since enabled her to give further evidence of her interest in the Irish dramatists by the production of such of their plays as could not obtain a hearing in Dublin.

The Irish National Theatre Society began the year 1904 in its old makeshift quarters where, nevertheless, two notable plays were produced, *The Shadowy Waters* by Yeats, and Synge's *Riders to the Sea*, before the Abbey Theatre was ready to receive them. In December, however, the Players were housed in their new home, and during the succeeding twelve months many valuable additions were made to their repertoire, including *The Well of the Saints*, by J. M. Synge, *The Land* by Padraic Colum, and *Spreading the News*, the first of those amusing farces which have constituted Lady Gregory's greatest success in the Theatre. By the end of the next year it was evident that the National Theatre had come to stay; new plays and new playwrights offered themselves in an abundance sufficient to indicate a wide response to the new stimulus, and there was no doubt but that Miss Horniman's experiment was in the process of being justified. To consecrate this promise of success, and to affirm, as it were, the official and national existence of the Dramatic Movement, there came the final form of that title whose variations, — from "W. G. Fay's Irish National Dramatic Company" to the "Irish National Theatre Society" — we have noticed. Henceforward the organization was known as the National Theatre Society. Thus, the Irish Literary Theatre prepared the way for the National Theatre, which was largely the creation of W. G. Fay. As Yeats wrote at the time in *Samhain:* "We owe our National Theatre Society to him and his brother, and we have always owed to his playing our chief successes."

If it be asked what was the special contribution of the Fays to the Theatre, the reply must be, the acting of the Irish Players. Wherever the latter have appeared, the peculiar quality of their art has not failed to draw forth much comment, whose terms have become familiar through the columns of a thousand newspapers and reviews. It will be enough to recall here in brief the characteristics of the so-called "Abbey Theatre school" of acting, as they have impressed the majority of critics, bearing in mind that their cultivation must be attributed to the Fays: to W. G. Fay, who long served as stage manager, and to Frank Fay, whose study of diction made him the natural teacher of his comrades. Both brothers had found in French acting the model which was at once the most perfect manifestation of the art, and that most removed from the histrionic methods of the English stage. Hence, no doubt, the surprise, to English-speaking audiences, of the performances given by the Irish Players, where the unusual nature of the plays themselves was heightened by the un-English manner of their interpretation.

The acting of the Players trained by Fay bore many traces of the model by which it was inspired, and we need not be surprised to hear that Frank Fay had amassed a most extraordinary collection of books

dealing with the art of speaking, mainly French works.
W. B. Yeats at once recognized a certain similarity
between the players of the Théâtre Français and those
of the Irish company, as an early issue of *Samhain*
shows. There we find him attributing — wrongly as
it happened — to the example of de Max and Sarah
Bernhardt in *Phèdre*, some of the effects which had
pleased him in Fay's work. The latter had not seen
the performance in question, but he had absorbed at
the fountain-head the science and art which had gone
to make that performance, and thousands like it, a
charm for the eye and ear. The stage grouping by
which the actors were taught to efface themselves, in
order that attention should be concentrated upon the
speaker, was one of the lessons imparted by French
tradition to the Irish Players. From the same teacher
they learned to dispense with those absurd movements
and gestures into which the delivery of a sustained
speech seems to galvanize popular English actors.
Further, in truly French fashion, the Players were
made to realize that even the most minor part is important, and must be interpreted with the same care
and skill as the principal rôle. The absence of the
"star" system facilitated this, as the same performer
would be given parts of the most varied importance,
and could count upon as much appreciation in a subordinate as in a more prominent rôle. Another consequence of this condition was that the scene could not
be given exclusively to a display of one talent in the
company, as is the case when the actor-manager
favorite performs for the gratification of his admirers.

Many other innovations were made, which have since become commonplaces by reason of the increase of "little theatres", where the production of literary drama has made necessary the abolition of a system incompatible with any art more serious than that of the *matinée* idol. The most important factor in the work of the Irish Players, however, was elocution, to which Frank Fay brought the fruits of his deep study of the French masters, and the practical demonstration of his own beautiful voice as he had developed it. It will be remembered that what at once captured Yeats in the Fays' company was their power to give full effect to spoken verses, and he has frequently expressed his personal debt to Frank Fay for the manner in which the latter has rendered the lines of the poet's own contributions to the repertory of the National Theatre. The soft rhythmic speech and delicate intonation of the Irish Players has added immeasurably to the appeal of the Irish playwrights, whether in prose or verse, and has made comprehensible the profound poetry of the Anglo-Irish idiom to those unacquainted with the language as spoken. So perfectly did Fay consummate the harmony of idiom and diction that even Mrs. Patrick Campbell did not prove a wholly successful interpreter of Yeats's *Deirdre*, when she played the title part in London. Miss Sara Allgood, in the subordinate rôle of the chief musician, attracted greater praise, thus procuring most striking and impartial testimony to the genius of the teacher by whose methods she was taught.

By a happy chance W. G. Fay's talent lay in comedy,

while his brother's gift was in the interpretation of poetic drama. While Frank Fay created the parts of Forgael in *The Shadowy Waters*, of Seanchan in *The King's Threshold*, of Naisi in *Deirdre*, and of Cuchulain in *Baile's Strand*, W. G. Fay infused his comedic spirit into the central figures of Synge's comedy, playing the Tramp in *The Shadow of the Glen*, Martin Doul in *The Well of the Saints*, and Christy Mahon in *The Playboy of the Western World*. In this way, Yeats and Synge were both in the fortunate position of having at their disposal perfect instruments for the expression of their respective geniuses. In Miss Moira O'Neill, Miss Maire nic Shiubhlaigh, and Miss Sara Allgood, not only Yeats and Synge in particular, but all the Irish playwrights of the first decade of the Dramatic Renascence, had interpreters whose skill in comedy was equaled only by their perfect mastery of speech and tragedy.

In recent years the tradition created by the original group has been carried on by Messrs. Sinclair, Kerrigan, O'Donovan, and Miss Eithne Magee — to mention the more important members of the present Abbey Theatre Company, who may be regarded as pupils of the brothers Fay. Nowadays the older players occasionally perform at the Abbey Theatre, but, in the main, the later dramatists depend upon actors whose accession to the company has coincided with their own appearance in the list of contributors to the repertory of the Theatre. A school of acting was organized four years ago in order to train new players in the tradition created by the Fays, and from this material

there have been drawn recruits who fill the gaps in the
ranks of the original company. Unfortunately, the
spirit of that tradition has tended to evaporate as
those who inspired it drifted away, and a stereotyped
style has replaced the spontaneity of old. In consequence, a certain disappointment has become perceptible in the comments which have greeted recent performances of the reconstructed company of Irish Players.
Critics are accusing both the actors and playwrights
of living upon the past reputation of the National
Theatre. When considering the work of the dramatists
in detail, we shall have occasion to notice this suspicion
of deterioration which attaches no less to the dramatic
literature itself, than to the conditions of its selection
and execution.

For the present it will suffice to say that the Irish
Dramatic Movement was turned into a channel which
flowed directly along the lines of national tradition,
when its most vital forces converged upon the point
of W. G. Fay's departure. It found through him the
maximum intensity of expression, in that his art was
precisely such as to stimulate the dramatization of the
most characteristic elements of Irish life, and to provide
the dramatists with an almost ideal vehicle of artistic realization. Poetic drama and folk-drama found
equally their impulse and encouragement in the plans
and methods whose ultimate justification was the birth
of a National Theatre, unique in the English-speaking
world. So closely related are players and playwrights
that it was frequently difficult to decide the just measure of credit due to each in their common triumph.

The comparative failure of foreign actors in Irish plays has already been alluded to, and finds its counterpart in the insignificance of the success obtained by such of the Irish Players as ventured into the English theatre of commerce. Before turning to the work of the dramatist whose literary ideals and practical idealism have meant so much to the Irish Theatre, it is interesting to place on record his theory of drama. The following extract from an early article by W. B. Yeats in the 1903 issue of *Samhain* will show how closely his program coincided with the intention of the Fays, and the realization of their purpose :

I think the theatre must be reformed in its plays, its speaking, its acting and its scenery. That is to say, I think there is nothing good about it at present.

First. We have to write or find plays that will make the theatre a place of intellectual excitement — a place where the mind goes to be liberated. . . . If we are to do this we must learn that beauty and truth are always justified of themselves, and that their creation is a greater service to our country than writing that compromises either in the seeming service of a cause. . . .

Second. If we are to restore words to their sovereignty we must make speech more important than gesture upon the stage. . . . An actor should understand how to so discriminate cadence from cadence, and to so cherish the musical lineaments of verse or prose that he delights the ear with a continually varied music. . . .

Third. We must simplify acting, especially in poetic drama, and in prose drama that is remote from real life like my *Hour-Glass*, we must get rid of everything that is restless, everything that draws the attention away from the sound of the voice, or from the few moments of intense expression, whether that expression is through the voice or through the hands. . . .

Fourth. Just as it is necessary to simplify gesture that it may accompany speech without being its rival, it is necessary to simplify both the form and color of scenery and costume. As a rule the background should be but a single color, so that the persons in the play, wherever they stand, may harmonize with it and preoccupy our attention. . . .

These lines are as fittingly a summary of the dramatic art of the National Theatre as they are an introduction to the writings of the poet who will always be entitled to the first place in any history of contemporary Irish drama.

CHAPTER IV

William Butler Yeats

1

Writing and Environment

I⊤ was not only a literary ideal, but also a literary generation, that separated the first and second phases of the Dramatic Revival in Ireland. W. B. Yeats was born in Dublin in 1865; he belonged, therefore, to that younger generation of poets and prose writers who attained manhood in the early "eighties", and initiated the movement commonly known as "the Celtic Renascence." He was the first of his contemporaries to obtain the recognition of a wide public, and he has come to be regarded as the embodiment of all that was, and is, represented by the Irish Literary Revival. George Moore affirmed in *Vale* that "all the Irish movement rose out of Yeats and returns to Yeats" — a somewhat loose way of indicating the predominant position of the poet in the history of modern Anglo-Irish literature. A recent biographer, Mr. Forrest Reid, elaborating the generalization still further in the direction of inaccuracy, actually concludes that "no other writer of first-rate importance" has been associated with the movement! The names of A. E., John Eglinton, and J. M. Synge, to mention only the more important of Yeats's companions, are enough to indicate the dangers of the enthusiastic method in literary criticism. It is true, however, that earlier fame confirmed Yeats in the leadership of a movement which he had from the beginning consciously directed. It was, therefore, a natural outcome of that leadership that he should have associated himself with the dramatic ideals of the new generation, rather than with those of his elders.

Six of Yeats's childhood years were spent in London, but at the age of fifteen he returned to Dublin, where he continued his education at the Erasmus Smith School, an institution where he formed the companionships which were to play an important part in the preparatory period of the Celtic Revival. His fellow pupils included several whose names were afterwards familiar to lovers of Irish poetry, — Charles Weekes, John Eglinton, and Charles Johnston. To these were added George W. Russell (A. E.), who joined the group which fought the political heresy of the time, namely, that patriotic verse was necessarily good poetry. Yeats, in particular, urged the claims of such poets as James Clarence Mangan and Samuel Ferguson, who had substituted the legends and lore of Ireland's antiquity for the rhetoric of aggressive nationalism. His success in this respect was such as to restore Irish poetry to literature, saving it from the semi-oblivion of political versification and song. Yeats imposed a new standard which was at once literary and national, and out of its adoption there grew that poetic flowering which constituted the chief distinction of the Celtic Renascence.

In 1889 Yeats published *The Wanderings of Oisin*, a volume in which he had collected the best of his contributions to the Irish reviews, and whose unusual qualities at once attracted attention, constituting it, as it were, the herald of the Literary Revival. With those exceptions, such of these poems as had previously been published were reprinted from Irish periodicals, *The Dublin University Review*, *The Irish Monthly*, and *The Irish Fireside*, but the year of their publication in book form marked the end of his first period of literary activity in Ireland. During the decade from 1889 to 1899 the poet resided chiefly in London (with occasional visits to Dublin and Paris) and almost all his work appeared in English newspapers and reviews. He became a member of the Rhymers' Club, forming with Lionel Johnson and John Todhunter the Irish contingent at that gathering which was the poetic center of London during the "eighteen-nineties." These were ten years of intense experience and constant work, during which Yeats steadily rose to the first rank among his English contemporaries. In 1892 he published *The Countess Cathleen and Various Legends and Lyrics;* in 1893, *The Celtic Twilight*, and in 1894 his first play, *The Land of Heart's Desire*, was produced at the Avenue Theatre. *The Secret Rose* came in 1897 to confirm the estimate of his powers as a delicate prose writer, which had been revealed in *The Celtic Twilight*. Meanwhile he had been busy as an editor and journalist, editing various collections of fairy stories, compiling that useful anthology, *A Book of Irish Verse* (1895), and collaborating in the sumptuous three-volume edition of Blake, issued in 1893 by Bernard Quaritch. His own book of collected *Poems* appeared in 1895, and gave a complete survey of his verse from the beginning, in 1889. Four years later a revised edition of this volume indicated the spread of the author's fame, which reached a definite stage when *The Wind Among the Reeds* (1899) closed a period in the evolution of the poet's talent.

This work was the culminating expression of a gradual preoccupation with the doctrine and speculations of mystic symbolism, which had first become noticeable in the revision and rearrangement of the verses which went to make up the 1895 edition of *Poems*. Direct contact with the English symbolists, and indirect association with the occultists and mystics of the French literature of the period, had led Yeats to elaborate the fund of natural mysticism which he brought with him to London. The simple mystic leanings of the Irish peasantry, illustrated in the lore of *The Celtic Twilight*, had become more conscious and more intellectual in the abstruse reveries of *The Secret Rose*, some of whose personages are transferred as weighty symbols to *The Wind Among the Reeds*. This little book, with its bulky glossary, is overburdened by a symbolism which essays to preach obscure doctrines whose clarity is by no means heightened by those pages of explanatory matter. Further progress in this direction was clearly impossible, for here the poet had reached the limit imposed by his vision. He had chastened and purified his verse, emptying it of all rhetoric only to find that in escaping the latter he had become involved in a process no less reprehensible. This very economy of words had given his poetry an inhuman abstractness which failed to convey its intellectual message. Withal, however, *The Wind Among the Reeds* achieved success by its subtle beauty. It was the over-refinement of Yeats's art which gave us the quintessence of his poetic spirit and terminated the stage of pure lyricism.

It was a happy coincidence that, at the moment when his lyric genius reached maturity, W. B. Yeats should have begun to turn his thoughts towards the theatre. *The Wind Among the Reeds* was issued in 1899, the year which gave birth to the *Irish Literary Theatre.* From that date up to the present time the energies of Yeats have been absorbed by the task of fostering in Ireland a national drama. He has not published a substantial volume of verse since, contenting himself with the preparation of the Collected Edition of his works in 1908, and the issue of occasional slender booklets of prose and poetry, privately printed by the handpress of his sisters at Dundrum, Ireland. Apart from these, and the revision of his earlier verse for new editions, all Yeats's original writings since 1899 have been destined for the stage or have been critical essays connected therewith. The effect of this constant participation in practical work and the necessity of complying with the exigencies of such an enterprise as the Irish Theatre, have not left the poet untouched.

The later verse of W. B. Yeats shows him concerned with contemporary Irish life, and less remote from the passions and emotions of his time. He is still charged with obscurity, rather in obedience to an accepted convention than because of any actual return to the symbolic elaborations of *The Wind Among the Reeds.* The allusions and references which he introduces into his impassioned comments upon the people and events of to-day in Ireland are elusive only to the most impatient reader. Most of his admirers cannot but be stirred by these recent evidences of the return of a great poet's imagination to the scenes and passions of his earliest inspirations. An examination of Yeats's non-dramatic writings since 1899 will show that the genius which can give us such poems as are found in *The Green Helmet* (1910) and *Responsibilities* (1914), — not to mention *In the Seven Woods* (1903) which has been reprinted in various collected editions, — must still be counted amongst the purest in modern Irish poetry. It is unjust and unfair to accuse Yeats, as so many have done, of impoverishing our lyric treasure by devoting the wealth of his mind to the theatre. His gifts to the former have been lavish, and are still precious, while he has enriched the latter in a measure far beyond that indicated by his own dramatic compositions.

We have seen how he turned to the theatre at the end of his richest period of lyrical inspiration, a fact which would alone suffice to justify the wisdom of such a choice. But it is a mistake to suppose that this was a sudden manifestation of an interest hitherto unsuspected. The earliest work of W. B. Yeats to be published in book form was *Mosada*, a dramatic poem, which appeared in 1886, and this had been preceded, in the pages of the *Dublin University Review*, by *The Island of Statues*, " an Arcadian Faery Tale " in two acts, and by *The Seeker*, a dramatic poem, in two scenes. Evidently as far back as 1885 the dramatic form had appealed to Yeats, even though he wrote with no thought of the stage. In 1892 his second volume of collected verse was published, with a play for its title piece, *The Countess Cathleen*, which was destined to be the inaugural production of the Irish Literary Theatre. Two years later, and five years before the latter event, the poet witnessed the first performance of his work upon the stage, when *The Land of Heart's Desire* was produced in London. Some critics have taken this to be the starting point of Yeats's ambition to create an Irish Theatre, but the facts seem rather to indicate it as the crystallization of a tendency long present in his work. It certainly disposes of the theory that Yeats was abruptly torn from his true vocation by the impetus of the Dramatic Movement.

Strict regard for the chronological method would impose the necessity of examining at this point the two plays just mentioned. They belong to a period anterior to the existence of the Irish Theatre, and do not seem to fall into the same category as their successors, which were written directly to meet the needs of that institution. Yeats himself has given the lead in this respect to many critics, who have classified his drama in accordance with his own selection. Twice he has divided his dramatic writings into two parts, giving the collec-

tive title, *Plays for an Irish Theatre*, to the work immediately connected with the Dramatic Movement in
Ireland. The first occasion was on the publication of
a series of five volumes — to which Yeats contributed
four and Synge one — during the years 1903 to 1907.
The second was in 1911, when he issued a volume of
his collected plays under that title, but his later choice
did not coincide exactly with that of the previous
collection.

The reason is not far to seek. All his writing for
the stage has been governed by the presence of
the Abbey Theatre, for which even his earlier work
has been fundamentally revised and rewritten. *The
Countess Cathleen* as performed by the Irish Players
in the version published in 1912 is by no means identical with the title piece of the 1892 volume of lyrics;
even the spelling of the name was altered on its second
publication! It is best to consider them in groups,
according to the nature of their inspiration. For this
we have the precedent of the author when arranging
his *Collected Works* in the eight-volume edition of 1908.
In that well-ordered presentation, the most satisfactory of the innumerable editions for which Yeats
is noted, the destination or purpose of the plays is not
the basis of titular differentiation. They are grouped
mainly by reference to an approximate identity of mood
or theme, without regard for chronology, the legendary
dramas being in an earlier volume than the others,
although of later conception. Here, however, we may
reverse this order, reserving for the end those plays
based upon the legends of Celtic history.

2

Miscellaneous Plays in Verse and Prose

The Countess Cathleen, as originally conceived, was a lyrical drama whose poetic content far outweighed its dramatic significance. Starting with a popular folk-tale, whose theme is common to all ancient literatures, Yeats had less care for its adaptability to the stage than for its potential beauties, as unfolded by a poet rapidly approaching complete mastery of his art. The story relates how, at a time of dire famine in Ireland, two evil demons come, in the guise of human beings, to tempt men and women to barter their souls for food. The unholy traffic proceeds until the Countess Cathleen is moved to offer all her wealth in order to save her people. But the demoniacal powers have stolen her money and held back her shiploads of grain, for their supreme ambition is to capture this noble soul. Their triumph seems assured, for in desperation Cathleen agrees to sell her soul to the demons, on condition that she thereby redeem the souls already lost to them, and obtain the means of supporting the starving population until relief is in sight. The bargain is made in good faith by the Countess Cathleen, who dies of grief in the realization of her sacrifice. Her soul, however, is saved, as in a final vision we see her carried up to heaven:

The light beats down: the gates of pearl are wide,
And she is passing to the floor of peace,
And Mary of the seven times wounded heart
Has kissed her lips, and the long blessed hair

> Has fallen on her face; the Light of Lights
> Looks always on the motive, not the deed,
> The Shadow of Shadows on the deed alone.

Yeats has given much time and care to the revision
of this play, infusing elements of a more dramatic life
into it, but at the expense of its early poetic beauty.
The subject is essentially alien to the modern stage,
however effective it might have been in the less sophisticated ages of allegory and morality plays. There is
something inherently incredible in the material repre-
sentation of the supernatural protagonists, who are
conceivable only to the eye of imagination. In spite
of all he has done to make *The Countess Cathleen* convincing in the theatre, Yeats cannot progress beyond
the limitations imposed by the theme itself, which is
too tenuous for such exploitation. Consequently, his
only reward is to find his critics regretting, at each revision, the disappearance of those beauties which made
the original version impressive. The truth is, that
early play, for all its faults of inexperience, had an
appeal which endures, so long as one is content to regard the work as a dramatized poem. A sense of terror
pervades the scene, as in those symbolistic dramas of
Maeterlinck, where mysterious forces manifest their
presence in the occurrence of simple, but significant,
incidents.

The barking of a dog, a hen fluttering in fear of the
unseen, the sight of two horned owls before the window,
— these are the portents of impending evil, confirmed
by reports of strange phenomena: "a woman met a

man with ears spread out, and they moved up and down like wings of bats"; a herdsman saw "a man who had no mouth, nor ears, nor eyes, his face a wall of flesh." Finally, when the holy shrine falls from its niche, Shemus cries, as he crushes it under foot:

> The Mother of God has dropped asleep,
> And all her household things have gone to wrack.

A fitting moment for the entry of the two soul merchants, who thereupon begin their work of damnation. By a thousand little touches Yeats contrives to create that atmosphere of suggestion and anguish in which the typical drama of symbolism evolves. But he does more; he transfigures the whole play by verbal felicities of the purest poetry: Cathleen's dying words:

> Bend down your faces, Oona and Aleel:
> I gaze upon them as the swallow gazes
> Upon the nest under the eave, before
> He wander the loud waters. . . .

or the famous song of Aleel:

> Impetuous heart, be still, be still:
> Your sorrowful love may never be told;
> Cover it up with a lonely tune.
> He who could bend all things to His will
> Has covered the door of the infinite fold
> With the pale stars and the wandering moon.

There are so many wonderful lines in *The Countess Cathleen* that brief quotation is perhaps worse than useless to convey an adequate idea of this beautiful little play, which has so unfortunately failed in its attempt to satisfy two wholly dissimilar audiences. It will always receive impatient criticism from those who are convinced *a priori* that Yeats is not a dramatist, and who dismiss contemptuously his stage demons with all the primitive mystery to which they are related. On the other hand, it will be praised by admirers of the lyric poet, while they bemoan the excisions of the dramatist engaged in making a play out of the material of an exquisite poem. There remains, however, a third class (in every sense of the word) of criticism, which may be mentioned as one of those literary curiosities, to whose continued existence exasperated national sensitiveness has proved most propitious.

It will be remembered that *The Countess Cathleen* was the piece with which the Irish Literary Theatre began its career in 1899. The event was marked by one of those demonstrations of æsthetic illiteracy which have from time to time conferred a certain notoriety upon works deserving of more serious fame. A politician, a cardinal, and a newspaper combined forces in order to stir up opposition to the play, on the ground that it was blasphemous and unpatriotic. The first charge was based upon the language of the demons, the second upon the theme itself. It was argued that no Irishwoman would sell her soul to the devil, and that the personages of the play, natural and supernatural, referred in too irreverent fashion to sacred subjects, particular offence being taken at the incident of the falling shrine already quoted. A number of Catholic students were induced to sign a protest, and the usual preparations for creating a disturbance in the theatre were made, so that the first performance was attended by a large body of police to quell the disturbers. Thus, the Irish Theatre was inaugurated in circumstances which were to be repeated in its hour of greatest success, when rioting greeted the production of J. M. Synge's *The Playboy of the Western World*. It then became evident that the type of critic who could dismiss *The Countess Cathleen* as "a ridiculous and offensive absurdity" was not yet extinct, although happily he has consistently failed to alter the course of the Irish Literary Revival.

If frequent production be the test of popularity, then *The Land of Heart's Desire* is Yeats's most successful appeal to the playgoer. It was not only, as has been stated, the first of his plays to be performed, but was also the means of his introduction to the American stage in 1901. Here again the poet found his theme in folklore, the motive being contained in the introductory chapter to Yeats's *Fairy and Folk Tales of the Irish Peasantry*, where he says: "On Midsummer Eve, when the bonfires are lighted on every hill in honour of St. John, the fairies are at their gayest, and sometimes steal away beautiful mortals to be their brides." The little drama takes place in the kitchen of Maurteen Bruin and his wife, Bridget, whose son has just brought home his newly-married bride. Shawn's young wife, Mary, is portrayed as a delicate, fanciful girl, whose thoughts are with her book of legends, rather than with the housewifely duties of her new state. Bridget appeals to the priest to dissuade Mary from her reading, but the latter is fascinated by the fairy tale of Princess

Edain, who heard a voice singing on May Eve, and followed it until she came to the land:

> Where nobody gets old and godly and grave,
> Where nobody gets old and crafty and wise,
> Where nobody gets old and bitter of tongue.

The conversation then turns upon the fairies, and Mary Bruin is warned of the dangers which beset her this Midsummer Eve, but she is heedless of advice, and even cries to the fairies to take her. Unwittingly she has placed herself in their power by giving fire and food to several mysterious callers, whom the older folk recognize as emissaries of "the good people." Eventually she repents of her willfulness, but it is too late. Mary is glamoured by the singing of a little child who, having entered the kitchen, is gradually revealed, by various signs, as not of this world. She cannot, for example, bear the sight of a crucifix hanging on the wall, and not until Father Hart has removed it does she begin to exercise fully her magic power. With dancing and song the fairy child fascinates the soul of Mary Bruin, while the terror-stricken peasants gather about the priest, who is powerless in the absence of the crucifix. The spirit of yet another mortal is lured away to the "land of Heart's Desire", and Shawn is left with the lifeless body of Mary in his arms.

Out of this perfect little folk tale Yeats has made a symbolical drama of great beauty of language and execution. Prior to its revision in 1912, *The Land of Heart's Desire* was a prolonged delight to the ear by reason of the continuous music of its verse, which corresponded so intimately to the "drama-laden mood" of the play. Something of this quality has been lost in remodelling the lines to secure a greater degree of dramatic effectiveness. But there is still a wealth of poetry to enhance the effect of this fable which tells of the nostalgia of a soul for the Beyond, once it has glimpsed in vision the magic world of the spirit. The tedium of human life has seized upon Mary Bruin, and all her thoughts are concentrated upon the distant land of enchantment, which is revealed to her, in truly Celtic fashion, by the whispering of the wind through the forests and the waters lapping on the lake shore. Yeats has often sung of this, as have many Irish poets, — Nora Hopper in her *Fairy Music*, James Cousins in *The Bell Branch*, Thomas Boyd in *To the Leanán Sidhe*. The burden of their song is in the lines which close the play:

The wind blows out of the gates of the day,
The wind blows over the lonely heart,
And the lonely of heart is withered away,
While the fairies dance in a place apart,
Shaking their milk-white feet in a ring,
Tossing their milk-white arms in the air;
For they hear the wind laugh and murmur and sing
Of a land where even the old are fair,
And even the wise are merry of tongue;
But I heard a reed of Coolaney say:
"When the wind has laughed and murmured and sung
The lonely of heart must wither away."

The revised version of *The Land of Heart's Desire*, as it was revived at the Abbey Theatre in 1911, has been the subject of some adverse criticism, but the complaints have all had a literary basis. Indignation is expressed at the manner in which beautiful passages have been suppressed, whereas there was a time when morality, not poetry, was the question at issue between Yeats and his critics. In 1904 a booklet by a Mr. F. H. O'Donnell was issued, under the title, *The Stage Irishman of the Pseudo-Celtic Drama*, in which the work and motives of W. B. Yeats, Edward Martyn, and their colleagues were impugned in a manner only comparable to the hysterical manifestations of the anti-Synge campaign. Indeed, Mr. O'Donnell's effort would not deserve exhumation were it not that he represented an attitude of mind with which the Irish Theatre had to contend, and whose disappearance must largely be attributed to the steadfast purpose of Yeats and his supporters. His pamphlet may, therefore, be of some pathological interest to the American public, which has to-day more frequent opportunity than is fortunately possible in Ireland to observe the same influences at work.

Mr. O'Donnell devotes many pages to collecting and elaborating the abusive criticism which greeted *The Countess Cathleen*, and then turns his attention to *The Land of Heart's Desire*. It is described as "another revolting burlesque of Irish Catholic religion", and is, we are informed, even worse than its predecessor, being "instinct with dechristianisation!" If the specific object of this wrath be sought, it would appear to be the incident of the removal of the crucifix by Father Hart. This "blasphemous twaddle", as the scene is elegantly designated, affected certain hyper-sensitive persons exactly as did the falling shrine in *The Countess Cathleen*. Yet, as we have seen, both were part of a series of premonitions, announcing the approach of some supernatural event, in the manner now most readily associated with the dramas of Maeterlinck. The author of the pamphlet, however, with the characteristic obtuseness of the class whose spokesman he is, can see in these intrinsically unimportant incidents nothing short of a deliberate onslaught upon Christian beliefs. The chauvinists, moral and political, of Irish criticism have never departed from this line of attack, and *The Stage Irishman of the Pseudo-Celtic Drama* contains the quintessence of their intolerant spirit. It may be recommended to the cynical, for there they will find, some years before the event, all the stock "arguments" with which *The Playboy of the Western World* was so noisily belabored: the knowing references to "Baudelairian", "decadent French" influences, the moral vaporings and the patriotic indignation. It is strange to reread the phrases which, so freely applied to the ironic extravaganza of Synge, had also served to excite prejudices against the two poetic fantasies of the genius most remote from his. Yeats is fortunate, indeed, in that his recent critics have challenged his judgment upon points which are at least within the scope of intelligent discussion.

It is an interesting fact that the most intensely dramatic play which Yeats has written for the Irish Theatre should be the little "one-acter", *Cathleen ni Houlihan*. This was the companion piece to A. E.'s

Deirdre, when W. G. Fay's company inaugurated the second phase of the Theatre in April, 1902, and it is one of those rare cases in which the author has succeeded in pleasing all critics, not excluding the extremists, to whom reference has just been made. A further interest is lent to the circumstances of this success by reason of its being Yeats's first prose play. It was published in the issue of *Samhain* for October, 1902, and appeared in book form before the end of that year. A few months later, in dedicating the series of *Plays for an Irish Theatre* to Lady Gregory, the author made public some facts concerning *Cathleen ni Houlihan* which serve to explain the unique position it holds in Yeats's dramatic writings:

"One night I had a dream, almost as distinct as a vision, of a cottage where there was well-being and fire-light and talk of marriage, and into the midst of that cottage there came an old woman in a long cloak. She was Ireland herself, that Cathleen ni Houlihan for whom so many songs have been sung, and about whom so many stories have been told, and for whose sake so many have gone to their death. I thought if I could write this out as a little play, I could make others see my dream as I had seen it, but I could not get down out of that high window of dramatic verse."

We learn, then, that with Lady Gregory's collaboration, Yeats was able to give his dream the form he desired, "the country speech" which he lacked being supplied out of her experience of the Galway peasantry.

The play follows closely the vision of the poet, relating how Peter and Bridget Gillane have prepared for the wedding of their son, Michael, which is to take place on the morrow. A stranger enters the cottage in the midst of these preparations, an old woman, worn out with much wandering, and craving hospitality. She has been driven out on to the roads of the world by "too many strangers in the house", and the loss of her "four beautiful green fields", and in crooning song she tells of the great events in her history. Her story exercises a strange fascination upon Michael, who hears of the great men who have died for Cathleen, and longs to serve her. The old woman warns him :

It is a hard service they take that help me, many that are red-cheeked now will be pale-cheeked ; many that have been free to walk the hills and the bogs and the rushes, will be sent to walk hard streets in far countries ; many a good plan will be broken ; many that have gathered money will not stay to spend it ; many a child will be born and there will be no father at its christening to give it a name. They that had red cheeks will have pale cheeks for my sake ; and for all that, they will think they are well paid.

Cathleen goes out singing, and a few moments later the arrival of the French ships in Killala Bay is announced. Michael Gillane, forgetting his wedding and the ties of friends, follows her, having resolved in his turn to give up all in the service of nationality. The spirit of Ireland is revitalized by such sacrifices as these, for as the curtain falls, we hear no longer of an old woman ; Cathleen ni Houlihan has become "a young girl" with "the walk of a queen."

The poignancy of this little tragedy never fails to

touch an Irish audience, and the play enjoys the distinction of being the only work of Yeats which is more effective in the theatre than in the printed book. Its appeal was greatly enhanced, on the occasion of the first performance, by the presence of Miss Maude Gonne in the title part. Her personality lent a particular significance to this poetization of a political history with which she was so intimately and passionately associated. Yeats has placed on record a touching tribute to this interpretation of his thought: "Miss Maude Gonne played very finely, and her great height made Cathleen seem a divine being fallen into our mortal infirmity." "It was a fine thing," he wrote in *Samhain* after the performance, "for so beautiful a woman to consent to play my poor old Cathleen, and she played with nobility and tragic power." He contrasts her acting and that of her successors in the rôle with the unfortunate innovations of certain actresses on this side of the Atlantic. "The part has been twice played in America by women who insisted on keeping their young faces, and one of these, when she came to the door, dropped her cloak, as I have been told, and showed a white satin dress embroidered with shamrocks!" For the information of those interested he adds: "The most beautiful woman of her time, when she played my Cathleen, 'made up' centuries old, and never should the part be played but with a like sincerity."

Cathleen ni Houlihan, not being a drama of heroic legend like the *Deirdre* of A. E. which preceded it, was therefore the earliest occasion for the display of those histrionic qualities which the Fays were fostering and developing in their dramatic company. Here, for the first time, was an opportunity to interpret a play in the "folk-manner", later so celebrated amongst the achievements of the Irish Players. Yeats has testified that in the *Countess Cathleen* the way "of quiet movement and careful speech, which has given our players some little fame, first showed itself." And he concludes his commentary: "I cannot imagine this play, or any folk play of our school, acted by players with no knowledge of the peasant, and of the awkwardness and stillness of bodies that have followed the plough, or too lacking in humility to copy these things without convention or caricaturing." While the subsequent collaborations of W. B. Yeats and Lady Gregory have failed to please all but a few critics, this initial experiment was singularly happy in its results. If it has not proved so fortunate in its ultimate development, it furnished compensation by serving to crystallize the tradition of acting which is the invaluable gift of the Fays to the Dramatic Movement in Ireland.

Perhaps the most remarkable instance of the collaboration of Lady Gregory and Yeats, and its result, is furnished by *Where there is Nothing*. This work was originally published in 1903, as the first volume of *Plays for an Irish Theatre*, but curious to relate, it was produced by the London Stage Society, and has never been part of the Abbey Theatre repertory. The play performed there in 1907 was a rehandling of Yeats's subject by Lady Gregory under the title *The Unicorn from the Stars*. It is this latter version which Yeats has included in his *Collected Works*, the original play having been utterly discarded by him. In thus belying the series which it so inappropriately opened, *Where there is Nothing* naturally excites curiosity as to the reason of its appearance and subsequent abandonment. In his preface to *The Unicorn from the Stars* in 1908, the author hinted at some mystery, when he said that the earlier play has been written in a fortnight, in order to "save from a plagiarist a subject that seemed worth the keeping till greater knowledge of the stage made an adequate treatment possible." What was the precise scope of this allusion we do not know, but the speed and general circumstances of the play's construction sufficiently explain why it does not figure in later editions of Yeats's works.

Nevertheless, *Where there is Nothing* is very far from being an inconsiderable piece of hasty writing, and most readers will regret that he did not retain, and himself revise, this analysis of the revolt of the spirit against convention. Paul Ruttledge is a wealthy young landowner who abandons his money and position to join a band of vagrant tinkers. His delicate constitution is not fitted for the life of these hardy wanderers, so he falls ill, after many curious experiences and adventures. In the monastery where he is nursed, the mystic qualities in his nature are awakened by the presence of religion. Ruttledge joins the order in the hope of finding that Nirvana where finite and infinite are merged, and the soul of man is at peace. The brethren are swayed by his transcendental preaching and share his desire for that condition "where there is nothing that is anything and nobody that is anybody", for "where

there is nothing, there is God." The frenzy of his exaltation is contagious, and he finishes by bringing the
rank and file of the order to a state bordering on religious anarchism. The great sermon in which he
advocates a mystical iconoclasm, whose destructive
fury must not spare even the church itself, proves,
however, too great a trial of the Superior's patience.
Ruttledge and his disciples are ejected from the monastery, and finally fall victims to the fury of the peasantry, who cannot appreciate these excesses of Christian virtue. But the outcasts were already on the way
of destruction because of their failure to agree to the
intransigeant teaching of their leader. Ruttledge's
mystic ecstasy at the thought of death was beyond the
imagination of his companions, who opposed his passive
resignation by attempts to compromise with reality,
to the extent, at least, of keeping life in their bodies
by active work amongst the peasant population.

With the single exception of his early story, *John
Sherman* (1891), Yeats's only portrayal of contemporary
manners is in the opening scenes of *Where there is
Nothing*. There is a certain note of social protest and
criticism, such as one finds in Wilde and Bernard Shaw,
in the description of Paul Ruttledge's conventional surroundings, his commentary thereon, and the motives
of his revolt. The first three acts have a basis of action in the affairs of everyday life which, apart from
their intrinsic interest, add to the thoughtful fantasy
of the two remaining acts, whose interest centers about
the monastery and its scenes of spiritual delirium. In
The Unicorn from the Stars, this contrasted appeal is

lacking. The interest of such a protagonist as Paul
Ruttledge lay, to a great extent, in the circumstance
of his aristocratically useless existence and his reactions
against it. Lady Gregory's Martin Hearne, the coach-
builder, is a figure of much less significance, and the
satire of the earlier play finds no occasion for its exercise in her presentation of the unaltered theme.
Hearne's frenzy is produced by a vision beheld while
he is in a trance, induced by the flashing of light on a
golden unicorn which he has made to ornament a car-
riage. He too conceives a mission of destruction which
is carried out by almost the same agencies as in the
original story. Yeats had not only tacitly avowed his
belief in the superiority of the later play by incorporat-
ing it into his works, but he has recorded his estimate
of Lady Gregory's reconstruction of the material in the
following terms:

She has enabled me to carry out an old thought
for which my own knowledge is insufficient, and to com-
mingle the ancient phantasies of poetry with the rough,
vivid, ever-contemporaneous tumult of the roadside;
to create for a moment a form that otherwise I could
but dream of . . . an art that prophesies though
with worn and failing voice of the day when Quixote
and Sancho Panza long estranged may once again
go out gaily into the bleak air.

We know that *Where there is Nothing* was written with
the occasional help of two collaborators, of whom Lady
Gregory was one, and to that extent she may, indeed,
be responsible, as Yeats says, for the execution of his
plan. But since that play, unlike the subsequent

version, was issued in his name only, we may assume it to have been essentially his own conception. It would seem, therefore, more just to apply the eulogy above quoted, to *Where there is Nothing*, for it fits that play a great deal better than it does *The Unicorn from the Stars*. There is almost nothing of Yeats in the latter, whereas the former, for all its hasty construction, is entirely worthy of the poet, whose own voice is so often heard in the rebellious utterances of Paul Ruttledge. In the rewriting, all the elements of intellectual and spiritual revolt, which dominated the incoherencies of the original five acts and made them acceptable, are lost in the not too well-ordered logic of a conventional three-act drama. The appeal is transferred from the depths to the surface of the spectator's mind.

Apparently with some intention to duplicate the success of the little folk tragedy, *Cathleen ni Houlihan*, Yeats contributed, with Lady Gregory's assistance, a folk comedy entitled *The Pot of Broth* to the second season of W. G. Fay's Dramatic Company. Although both these plays were produced in 1902, it was not until 1904 that *The Pot of Broth* was published, when the author collected three one-act pieces for the second volume of *Plays for an Irish Theatre*. Like *Where there is Nothing*, it was not included in any edition of Yeats's collected works, after its appearance in that series, so that critics have frequently referred to it as having been disowned. But that is not strictly true, as *The Pot of Broth* was republished in separate form as late as 1911. However, this fact does not imply any superiority over the play which has really been denied by its author. *The Pot of Broth* is obviously the work of Lady Gregory rather than of Yeats, being nothing more than a trifling farce in the typical vein of her *Seven Short Plays*. A loquacious beggar succeeds in wheedling a credulous peasant woman into giving him all the ingredients for the making of broth, while convincing her that the food has been miraculously extracted from a magic stone placed by him in the pot. The broad comedy of the dialogue constitutes the play, the forerunner of those numerous farces which the talent of the Irish Players made it possible for Lady Gregory to write. W. G. Fay's creation of the tramp's rôle was largely responsible for a success which has since been repeated in similar pieces, thanks to a like coöperation on the part of the actors.

Before we come to the poetic plays of Irish legend, a point of transition is supplied by *The Hour Glass*, a morality, based upon a folk story which had attracted the attention of Yeats so far back as 1888, when he compiled his *Fairy and Folk-Tales of the Irish Peasantry*. It was first published and performed in 1903, as a prose play, but in spite of its having "converted a music-hall singer and kept him going to mass for six weeks", the author was not satisfied until he had rewritten it partly in verse. In 1914, this new version formed part of the volume *Responsibilities*, to which a characteristic note was added by way of an appendix. Emphasizing his distaste for didacticism, the poet described himself as but "faintly pleased" by the conversion of the vaudeville artist, "so little responsibility does one feel for that mythological world." On the other hand, he adds, "I was always ashamed when I saw friends of my own in the theatre." While noting the repudiation of moral, in favor of artistic, purpose, we shall respect the latter by considering *The Hour Glass* in its final, if not yet widely familiar, form.

The characters are the traditional personifications of the medieval morality: the Wise Man, representing science; the Fool, intuition; and the Pupils, the common herd of small, docile souls enslaved to formulæ. The Wise Man has devoted his years of learning to a denial of the invisible world, but, in contradiction of his reason, his spirit has passed on to him premonitions of the phenomena he denies. When his pupils come with a passage for him to elucidate and refute, in the light of the theories they have imbibed, the Wise Man is troubled. He has lost some of that positive assurance which gave weight to his negation of the soul, and soon his sensations of a life beyond materialize in the shape of an Angel, who warns him that death will come when the sands of the hour glass have run out. If he can find "but one soul that still believes that it shall never cease", he may find peace hereafter. In vain he searches for some trace of belief in those about him; the scientific rationalism of the Wise Man has extirpated faith in those whom he implores to no purpose. Teigue the Fool alone has escaped the teaching whose results are so tragically evident to the mind of the doomed man. The latter kneels at the feet of Teigue and entreats him to acknowledge the beliefs which so often transpired from his instinctive babbling. The Fool is intent upon more trivial things, and not until it is too late does he come, ready to confess his faith. In the last agonizing moment, however, the Wise Man recognizes the futility of his quest; he realizes that the better part is submission to the will of God, and that therein lies true wisdom.

As now published, *The Hour Glass* is one of the most remarkable moralities of modern literature, so perfectly has Yeats sensed the spirit of that form. When compared with *The Fool of the World,* his superiority over Arthur Symons is evident; when compared with his own earlier version, the beauty of the revised work gains additional force. Not only is the form embellished by what he terms "the elaboration of verse", but structurally the fable is more convincing. Originally the Wise Man was saved by the ingenuous confession of the Fool, a verbal fidelity to the text of the folk story which did not carry the naïve charm of the latter into the theatre. Now, however, instead of that "platitude on the stage", of which Yeats complained, he has projected a more faithful image of his own thought into a theme which still preserves the simple dignity befitting its medieval setting. Rarely have the revisions of Yeats been so immeasurably to the advantage of his work as in this carefully rewoven fabric of words, whose art is concealed by the perfect simplicity of their arrangement. Only transposition and analysis reveal the technical purity of a style unlike that of any other of his plays in prose or verse. A limpid clarity of vision is coupled with a symmetry of language, which secures a maximum of poetic effect with a minimum of specific verbal ornamentation.

3

Plays of Gaelic Legend and History

Of the five dramas whose material derives from the legendary lore of Gaelic Ireland, *The Shadowy Waters* is not only the earliest, but it was probably one of the first conceptions of the young poet. In his recent chapter of autobiography, *Reveries over Childhood and Youth*, Yeats tells of a boyish escapade, undertaken "to find what sea birds began to stir before dawn", which bears testimony to the priority of this play in his poetic meditations. He says: "It was for the poem that became fifteen years afterwards 'The Shadowy Waters' that I wanted the birds' cries, and it had been full of observation had I been able to write it when I first planned it." Two versions were planned and rejected, however, before Yeats was satisfied to make his work public, and even then he was not content until he had completely transformed it.

The Shadowy Waters was first published in *The North American Review*, in May, 1900, and was issued with slight modifications in book form the same year. This beautiful poem, obviously conceived without much thought for the exigencies of dramatic production, was performed by the Irish National Theatre Society in 1904. Its stage success was slight, although its poetic qualities have preserved for it a paramount place in the affection of Yeats's admirers. He himself declared that the 1904 performance of *The Shadowy Waters* was an "accident", due no doubt to his absence in America. On his return he proceeded to rewrite the play in the form published in 1906, and subsequently adopted for the Collected Edition of his works. The second, like the first published version, was in verse, but in spite of many — too many, some say — concessions to the demands of the theatre, a condensed "acting version" was found necessary. The latter is so evidently a makeshift that we may expect the poet to return to the subject. A series of attempts may yet indicate Yeats's desire to endow the Irish stage with a worthy interpretation of a thought upon which his imagination has brooded since boyhood.

Meanwhile we must content ourselves with the play which has received at least the measure of approval implied by its inclusion in the Collected Edition of 1908. The fundamental idea, so perfectly elaborated in the original poem, is here unchanged. Forgael, in quest of his ideal, has sailed the shadowy waters for three moons, his only guide the gray birds, voices of the ever-living. His crew rebel at this prolonged search in waste seas, where no chance of plunder falls to them, and ask Aibric to be their captain, in place of Forgael, whom they propose to kill. Aibric's loyalty to his friend forbids his joining in their plot, but even his faith is strained by the apparent fruitlessness of Forgael's cruise. He confesses his doubts to the latter, who is thereby afforded an opportunity to voice the idealism of the poet's dream. He describes the impulse which has led him to seek the woman whose perfect love shall bring them to "a place in the world's core where passion grows to be a changeless thing." While Forgael expounds his belief against Aibric's skepticism, his desire not to "linger wretchedly among substantial things", another ship is sighted. The sailors are overjoyed at the prospect of booty, and soon the strange vessel and its occupants are in their power. Amongst their prisoners is Queen Dectora, who demands satisfaction from those who have just slain her husband.

Forgael, whose thoughts are full of his ideal, is disappointed that fate should thus bring him but a mortal woman. His mysterious speech baffles and enrages Dectora, who calls upon the sailors to kill him, offering an immediate return home as their reward. But all are cast into spell by the magic breathings of Forgael's harp, and when Dectora comes to herself, she is conscious of a love for him whose advances she repulsed. Forgael's divine ecstasy, however, is still incomprehensible to her, and she now pleads that they return together. He cannot disregard the voices of his vision, urging him onward, and is resolved to abandon Dectora to Aibric, rather than forget the promise of ideal happiness. In a flash the woman senses the nobility of his purpose, and cutting the rope connecting the two galleys, allows the others to depart.

Dragon that loved the world and held us to it,
You are broken, you are broken. The world drifts
     away,
And I am left alone with my beloved,
Who cannot put me from his sight forever.

Thus the two spirits are united in the timeless region of immortality.

For all the changes *The Shadowy Waters* has undergone, the drama is essentially symbolical, and belongs definitely to the period of its first publication. Whatever that youthful poem may have been, for which Yeats studied the cries of the sea birds before dawn, its ultimate realization is far removed from such precision as that study implied. The symbolist poet of *The Wind Among the Reeds*, the mystic dreamer of *The Secret Rose*, is the author of this play, whose writing coincided with those volumes of his lyric maturity. It is informed by the same mood, and, in the 1900 version, it was a poem whose atmosphere was preserved by a perfect coincidence of thought and language. Hence the superiority of that first edition over those later experiments in dramatization, where effectiveness is so often substituted for original beauty.

While *The Shadowy Waters* is woven loosely out of legendary elements, Edain, the Celtic Aphrodite, and Ængus, the god of love, being among the protagonists, it was a play of symbolism rather than legend. It was followed, on the other hand, by a little tragedy taken directly from classic Gaelic literature, *On Baile's Strand*. As far back as 1892 Yeats had treated the theme of this play in a poem entitled *The Death of Cuchullin*, which has since been reprinted many times (with the inevitable variations in the spelling of Cuchulain's name!) but with few alterations in the text. Written in a harmonious arrangement of prose and verse, *On Baile's Strand* develops the familiar story of the tragic duel between Aoife's son, Finmol, and his unknown father, Cuchulain. In the early poem the father learns the identity of his adversary from the lips of the latter as he falls mortally wounded. A greater poignancy is achieved in the play by the introduction of the Blind Man and the Fool, whose comments, while the struggle is in progress, indicate them as possessing the knowledge denied to Cuchulain. These two serve throughout in the capacity of a Greek chorus, and through their indifferent chatter the father learns that he has slain his own child. He rushes out to die himself, battling with the waves, while the unwitting causes of his fatal enlightenment continue in their preoccupation with trivial things. The tragedy is one to which Yeats has given the imprint of his own personality, not only in the lovely lines of his verse, but in the characteristic rôle assigned to the crafty simpletons who are the mouthpieces of fate. Since its revision, after the opening performance of the Abbey Theatre, *On Baile's Strand* has become one of the author's most finished contributions to that repertory.

On its publication in the volumes of *Plays for an Irish Theatre* in 1904, it was accompanied by *The King's Threshold*, which had been produced in Dublin by the brothers Fay before the Players had secured a regular theatre. The plot is borrowed from a middle-Irish story of the demands of the poets at the court of King Guaire of Gort. Officials and ecclesiastics have combined to oust Seanchan, the poet, from the King's table, an affront which he resolves to avenge by starving on the steps of the palace; an old custom has it

> . . . that if a man
> Be wronged, or think that he is wronged, and starve

Upon another's threshold till he die,
The common people, for all time to come,
Will raise a heavy cry against that threshold,
Even though it be the King's.

The action, naturally, is constituted by the efforts of various people to dissuade the poet from his intention, but all fail to influence him, until finally the King is moved to make amends. He offers his own crown to Seanchan, who receives it only to return it to him whose kingship is demonstrably dependent upon the good will of the poets. Having vindicated his race, he is satisfied to renounce the mere symbol of royalty.

A personal interest attaches to *The King's Threshold* by reason of its having come at a time when hyper-sensitive patriotism was beginning its campaign against Synge, whose *Shadow of the Glen* had just excited the indignation of the political moralists. As Synge's sponsor, and because of his own offenses, Yeats's claims on behalf of art were being challenged. Whether intentionally or not, he here provided his critics with an answer which left no doubt as to his view of the relation that should exist between the poet and his public. A bitter note to a later edition of the play would seem to imply a deliberate purpose in its production, "when our Society was beginning its fight for the recognition of pure art in a community, of which one half is hired in the practical affairs of life, and the other half in politics and propagandist patriotism."

Almost every Irish poet has been drawn to the classical tragedy of Celtic epic history, the love-story of Deirdre and Naisi; A. E. wrote his prose poem upon the subject for the Fays, when they came forward to take the place of the Irish Literary Theatre, and four years later, in 1906, Yeats's version of the theme was given to the public, Frank Fay again playing the principal male part. A like period was to elapse before the third, and perhaps the greatest, of these modern dramatizations was made, — J. M. Synge's posthumous *Deirdre of the Sorrows*. Unlike A. E. and Synge, Yeats did not include the whole dramatic story, which tells of the lovers' flight to Alba, their sojourn, and the series of incidents which induced in Naisi the longing and finally the resolve to return home. He chose the last act of the tragedy, and made the arrival of Deirdre and Naisi at the palace of Conchubar his point of departure. While A. E.'s play presupposes an intimate acquaintance with the entire epic of the House of Usna, of which the Deirdre story is a part, Yeats has concentrated the tragic essence of the *dénouement* into a single act of great intensity.

The scene opens with a chorus of musicians, and Fergus as interlocutor. The latter has been instrumental in bringing Naisi and Deirdre to Conchubar, having guaranteed the good intentions of the King, whose revenge they suspect is lurking behind the invitation. The conversations of the musicians and Conchubar enable us to learn the events which have preceded the home-coming of the lovers, and the rapid narrative of the chorus brings about the mood of tension and expectancy necessary to the understanding of the play. We are prepared also, by the forebodings of the chorus, for the treachery of Conchubar, who has made use of

Fergus's friendship for Naisi to lure the latter into his power. Dark, sinister figures move furtively in the background, the air is filled with suspicion and hate, as innumerable insignificant happenings take on a dread significance in the light of what we hear of Conchubar. The doom of Naisi is being encompassed, the hired ruffians of the King lurk near to do his bidding, and only the renunciation of her lover by Deirdre can save him. She is willing to sacrifice herself, but Naisi forbids her and is murdered by Conchubar's servants. Then Deirdre, in a supreme moment of passion, feigns affection for the old King, who desires her, in order that she may be allowed to approach the dead body of Naisi. She goes behind the curtain where he lies and kills herself that she may be with him in death.

The inherent passion and tragedy in this great "sorrow of story-telling", as the Gaelic poets described it, are of themselves sufficient to give that grip and poignancy whose absence has been noted as a defect of the Yeatsian drama. Such human qualities as Yeats's *Deirdre* contains are not of his own contribution so much as a natural element in the epic literature of Gaelic Ireland. He resembles A. E. in his treatment of the subject, in so far as both have conceived the protagonists as figures of a dream rather than of reality. Technically, however, this work shows an advance upon the earlier poetic plays of Yeats. With a crisis in the affairs of Deirdre and Naisi as its starting point, it escapes that vague nervelessness which renders so much of the poet's writing ineffective on the stage. Were it not for the unusual possibilities of the theme, so finely realized by Synge, higher praise might be given to Yeats's version. As it is, the beauties of setting and language are such as to place *Deirdre* amongst the finest of the poet's creations.

In 1910 Yeats published a rewritten version of *The Golden Helmet*, which had been produced at the Abbey Theatre, Dublin, in 1908. In the revision the title was altered, becoming *The Green Helmet*, while a very novel experiment in the form was the use of ballad meter, instead of the original prose. This "heroic farce", as the author termed it, should serve as an introduction to the earlier play, *On Baile's Strand*. Its basis is the old story, known as *The Feast of Bricriu*, which Lady Gregory has included in her *Cuchulain of Muirthemne*. The Red Man, a spirit from the sea, has put the shame of cowardice upon Conall and Laegaire, by the exercise of his supernatural powers. The great hero Cuchulain, because of his innate valor and traditional courage, is alone capable of resisting the arts of the Red Man. He thereby gains the golden helmet as his reward, a gift which endows him with that heroic supremacy whose manifestations became the material of Gaelic epic.

The ancient bards conceived these figures as divine or semi-divine beings, whose virtue and nobility set them above humanity. In *The Green Helmet* we find a modern poet attempting, for the first time, to divest the heroes of the bardic imagination of their superhuman attributes. Humor is interjected into an atmosphere whose associations are of a very different character; and gentle satire is the result, — for example, the

jealous clash of ambitions, when the Red Man leaves the
golden helmet that it may be the cause of dissension
among the warriors. The familiar spirit of faction
which, as one of our poets has remarked, makes every
Irishman "a movement", is pleasantly symbolized by
the quarrel between Emer, Cuchulain's wife, Laeg,
his charioteer, and the women folk of Conal and
Laegaire. Perhaps a less fortunate innovation was
the use of ballad meter. But as an experiment in
the dramatization of the bardic material, this "heroic
farce" has a value of its own.

The announcement of a new play by W. B. Yeats,
The Player Queen, to be produced shortly in Dublin,
reminds us that for nearly ten years now his dramatic
writing has been in the nature of the revision. He has
been striving incessantly to reconcile his art as a poet
with the exigencies of the stage, and as we have seen,
hardly a play of his has been allowed to stand as first
performed and published. There can be no doubt of
his increased technical skill in surmounting the difficulties which stand in the way of success for such work
as his, when transferred to the theatre. Critics who regret the absorption of the poet by the dramatist profess
to see in every advantage of the latter some loss to the
former. They hold, in short, that the plays of Yeats
become dramatically effective at the expense of poetry.
While this may be true in a sense, the fact is of minor
importance. Poetic drama must combine, as its name
implies, the maximum of poetical effect with a maximum of dramatic significance, and the proportions of
both must be balanced. It is useless, therefore, to

complain that Yeats has, with increasing experience, been obliged to sacrifice something of his wealth of poetic beauty in order to secure a more dramatic effect. His early plays were so richly endowed with the former that harmony could be obtained only by the substitution of those qualities which he lacked. As he revises them they are less beautiful as poems, but more remarkable as poetic dramas.

The Irish Theatre owes so much to Yeats that we have some difficulty in assenting to the theory which condemns as fruitless his activities in that field. Not that the dramatists of the Revival have been his literary disciples, for the fact is Yeats is an isolated figure in the repertory of the Abbey Theatre. While the speaking of verse and the plastic beauty of dramatic art have interested him personally, the Theatre has become associated almost exclusively with realistic folk drama, and prose fantasies in the manner of Lord Dunsany. Gratitude for his share in fostering the revival must, therefore, be explained on more general grounds. His long and conscientious propaganda on behalf of artistic freedom, his complete devotion to the cause of national drama, resulting in the foundation of an institution unique in the English-speaking world — these are the realities which must prevent his contemporaries and successors from bewailing the potential loss to poetry involved by the deflection of his talents. We have noticed how the publication of *The Wind Among the Reeds,* on the eve of the Dramatic Movement, marked the limit of the poet's progress in the direction he had taken. For all his preoccupation with the drama,

Yeats has since found time for the expression of whatever lyric emotion has come to him. Some of his finest verse will be found in the pages of those little books which have been issued regularly from the Dun Emer and Cuala Press during recent years. Let us not be deceived by the too insistent regrets of those who ignore these later lyrics in the pleasing contemplation of what might have been.

When publishing in 1906 his first collection of poems since *The Wind Among the Reeds*, Yeats made a confession of literary faith, which remains, after all, the most conclusive commentary upon his work as a dramatist:

Some of my friends, and it is always for a few friends one writes, do not understand why I have not been content with lyric writing. But one can only do what one wants to do, and to me drama . . . has been the search for more of manful energy, more of cheerful acceptance of whatever arise out of the logic of events, and for clean outline, instead of those outlines of lyric poetry that are blessed with desire and vague regret.

He has here indicated not only the limitations which he felt had been imposed upon him by the development of his lyricism, but also the intention of his experiments in the theatre. If the plays of W. B. Yeats be compared with those of his contemporaries in England, France, Germany, or Italy, it will be found that he has earned his title to rank with the first of the poetic dramatists of to-day. The poetry of contemporary English literature in this respect is so lamentable that Ireland might well be content if Yeats were the only playwright of distinction associated with the National Theatre. The fact that his reputation has not been a matter of passing enthusiasm, as in the case of Stephen Phillips, that his work has found an audience increasingly capable of enjoying good drama in prose and verse, may be taken as doubly significant. Not only has his personal contribution to the Theatre been valuable, but his influence has created conditions propitious to the realization of his wider purpose. The play that is literature has found, not a small coterie but a public.

CHAPTER V

THE IMPULSE TO FOLK DRAMA: J. M. SYNGE AND PADRAIC COLUM

1

Writing and Environment

WHATEVER formative influence the work of W. B. Yeats might have had upon the younger dramatists of the Irish Theatre, had he continued to be the dominating literary personality of the movement, the fact now remains that the Irish drama has developed along very different lines. Here and there, as we shall see, one finds a play, or an isolated playwright like Lord Dunsany, whose affinity with the poetic drama conceived by Yeats is undeniable. But, in the main, the later dramatists derive from the tradition created by J. M. Synge and Padraic Colum. Both these writers were introduced to the public in 1903, during the first season of the newly constituted Irish National Theatre Society. Although Colum had been associated with the embryonic organization of the brothers Fay, from which the Society sprang, his real *début* may be said to have coincided with that of J.M.

Synge. The latter, having achieved in a few years
the fame which comes to others in a lifetime, occupied
that position of prominence in the Dramatist Revival
for which Yeats seemed destined. His influence,
therefore, dominated the subsequent evolution of Irish
drama.

Folk realism, however, while producing dramatic
literature of a texture most unlike the poetic woof of
Yeats's reveries, must not be regarded as a departure
from the ideals he had enunciated. The plays which
Yeats desired for the national stage should tell the
people of their own life, he postulated, "or of that life
of poetry where every man can see his own image,
because there alone does human nature escape from
arbitrary conditions." These words, written in anticipation of actual events, were clearly an invitation to
the exponents of peasant drama, and Yeats's champion-
ship of Synge subsequently demonstrated how genuine
was his wish to foster such art as is here predicted.
When he wrote thus in 1902 he must have been aware
of the quality of Synge's genius, which he had but
recently discovered, but it is doubtful if he could have
seen enough of the new dramatist's work to foretell
the destiny of the Irish Theatre. Yeats's plea may be
regarded, then, as a perfectly general statement of
a literary ideal, made without special reference to
Synge. It is all the more remarkable that a writer
should come into the movement equipped with every
advantage for the task of imposing the folk drama as
a powerful medium of national expression, and an
instrument of poetic and dramatic potency. The

classic genius of J. M. Synge conferred a prestige upon
the peasant play which seemed to justify the faith of
Yeats in the possibilities of a drama other than that
conceived by Edward Martyn. In another chapter
we shall have occasion to observe how the latter's
skepticism was also to be justified. For the present
it is enough to say that the Irish National Theatre
began its official career by making known the two most
original folk dramatists of our time.

Innumerable studies in periodical and book form
have so familiarized the public with the life and works
of J. M. Synge that little remains to be said. He was
born near Dublin in 1871, and studied at Dublin
University, to whose magazine *Kottabos* he contributed
his earliest literary effort, a sonnet published in 1893.
The same year he left college and began those *Wander-
jahre* in France, Germany, and Italy which terminated
about 1898, when he made the acquaintance of W. B.
Yeats in Paris. The latter at once recognized the unusual genius of the man, and convinced him that he
was wasting his talents in occasional journalism and
hack work of an unimportant character. Synge was
writing a little in French and English, travel sketches
and criticisms of French literature, but Yeats urged
him to return to Ireland and to seek his material
in the world of men, not of books. He went for six
weeks to the Aran Islands, and began to write the book
which, although it preceded his plays, was not published
until 1907, after much difficulty in finding a publisher.
This volume, *The Aran Islands*, was the fruit of many
prolonged sojourns among the islanders, and is a

document of great value to all students of Synge's work.

Once he had sensed the potentialities of his own country, Synge's visits to the continent of Europe became fewer. His years of vagabondage had given him just the preliminary training necessary to realize the opportunities offered by the study of elemental human activities in the last stronghold of our primitive national life. In the mountains of Wicklow and on those Western islands, Synge found the material of his art. His sympathies heightened by contact with the most varied phases of continental existence, his ears sharpened by attention to the shades and sounds of several European languages, he was particularly fitted to note the manifestations of peasant life in the idiom of the people. Unlike so many of his Irish contemporaries, he brought to the study of local conditions a mind well stored with foreign impressions, familiar with European culture, yet fundamentally colored by national traditions which his knowledge of Gaelic had preserved intact. Encouraged by Yeats, intensely moved by the spectacle of a primitive civilization unspoiled by industrialism, Synge consecrated his brief career to peasant Ireland. In *The Aran Islands*, the first of his notebooks, and in the posthumous volume, *In Wicklow, West Kerry and Connemara* (1910), will be found the rich store of observation and humanity which his years in Ireland brought to him. Out of this material were extracted the plays which have now made his name famous in several continents.

There is little of importance in the life of Synge to

be related in connection with his work for the Irish
Theatre. He was, as all who knew him have recorded, "a drifting, silent man", averse to discussion,
aloof from the controversies and activities of literature
in the making. It was an irony of fate that he precisely should become the center of the most violent
altercations in the field of politics and morality, and
finally be the rallying point for impassioned laudation
and depreciation of a literary *genre*. Biographically
the most remarkable feature of Synge's career was its
brevity. In the six years which elapsed between 1903,
when *In the Shadow of the Glen* was produced, to 1909,
when he died, he rose from absolute obscurity to world
fame, and provided us with the six plays upon which
his reputation must rest. His posthumously published
Poems and Translations (1909) are of interest, like
his notebooks, because of the insight they afford into
the application of his theories. Just as one may study
his sketches of life in the west of Ireland for the genesis
of his dramatic art, so one reads his versions of Villon
and Petrarch for their revelation of the poetic qualities
of Anglo-Irish idiom. Neither would in themselves
constitute a claim to public attention comparable to
that rightly accorded to his dramatic writings.

2

The Plays of J. M. Synge

In justice to the enemies of Synge it must be said
that from the beginning they left him under no illusions
as to the fate his plays would experience at their hands.

In the Shadow of the Glen, which marked his entrance
upon the stage of the National Theatre in 1903, was
greeted at once in the fashion which afterwards developed into the "Playboy riots." Although but a
variation upon a legend familiar to all folklore, this
little one-act play was repudiated by the moral patriots
as a hideous slander upon Irish womanhood. The
fable tells how an old farmer, Dan Burke, feigns death
in order to test the fidelity of his young wife, Nora.
As he lies stretched on his deathbed, he overhears the
conversation of Nora and a tramp whom she has admitted, his suspicions are aroused, and when his wife
goes out to bring in a neighbor in order to arrange for
the burial, he jumps up, to the intense horror and fear
of the tramp. Fortified with a drink of whisky, —
and his stick, — Dan resumes his position in the bed
and awaits the confirmation of his suspicions. Nora
returns with her friend, Michael Dara, and over a cup
of tea the pair discuss their marriage plans, and make
the most uncomplimentary allusions to the supposedly
dead husband. Dan's emotions are too strong for
him, so, with a violent sneeze, he awakes from the dead,
and drives his wife from the house, threatening both
her and Michael with his stick. The latter is a coward,
whose sole thought is to protect himself, his interest in
Nora having evaporated once it was evident she would
bring him no money. The tramp, however, willingly
accompanies Nora in her quest for the liberty of the
roads which he knows and loves so well. As they go
out of the house, the curtain falls on Dan and Michael
in complete harmony over a glass of whisky.

The play is a typically Syngesque combination of realism and symbolism. The legendary character of the plot is obvious, but the specific occasion of Synge's inspiration was undoubtedly a story told to him by Pat Dirane and recounted in *The Aran Islands,* though curiously enough, Pat's *dénouement* of murder and adultery is even more unfavorable to the illusions of Synge's critics. Similarly one may read into the play a criticism of the dowry system of loveless marriages, shared by Ireland with all peasant communities. Yet Nora is a figure transcending all such realistic interpretation. She is a symbol of a vigorous young woman mated, for reasons of property, with an old man, "wheezing, the like of a sick sheep." As she sees her lonely life passing away from her in the solitude of the isolated valley, lost in the mists from the hills, she is impelled to seek freedom and adventure. She escapes from the desolation of "hearing nothing but the wind crying out in the bits of broken trees left from the great storm, and the streams roaring with the rain."

Synge's next work was of very dissimilar character, although written about the same time as *In the Shadow of the Glen.* Unlike any other of his plays, except *Deirdre,* the poignant little tragedy, *Riders to the Sea,* met with the approval of all his critics. At least, none but a few minor technical objections have been raised against it. It was produced in 1904, and the following year the two one-act plays were issued in book form, the author's first contribution to permanent literature. *Riders to the Sea,* like its predecessor, had its roots in certain experiences recorded in *The Aran*

Islands, but not in any specific incident reported by the author. It might be said to concentrate within a small space the essential spirit of that work, which is, at bottom, a narrative of the constant struggle of the islanders against their relentless enemy, the sea. The womanhood of the Islands speaks through the tragic figure of old Maurya, who has lost her husband and four sons by drowning. When the scene opens she is waiting for news of her fifth son, Michael, who is missing, and whose fate is revealed by a young priest who brings portions of clothing, found on a drowned man, for Maurya's daughters to identify. They recognize their brother's clothes and conceal them from the mother, but try to prevent the last son, Bartley, from setting out in the storm to make the dangerous crossing to the mainland. Bartley refuses to be dissuaded, and rides off on his horse to the sea, without a fear for his fate. The inevitability of Greek tragedy weighs upon the scene, and numerous apparently trifling incidents emphasize the approaching doom of the son, whose mother sees in vision the realization of her forebodings. The old woman sings the *caoin,* or death-lament, of her lost sons, the wailing is taken up by the others, and when the dead body of Bartley is carried in, the cry of pain rises to passionate intensity, only to die away in a key of resignation even more terribly sad. "There isn't anything more the sea can do to me" is the submissive comment of Maurya.

There are few more flawless tragedies than this little piece, with its subtle blending of diverse elements, from the realism of the cottage interior, displaying an intimate knowledge of Aran customs, to the symphonic quality of the appeal to the ear in the phrasing of the speeches and the wonderful diapason of the *caoin*. Describing a burial in one of his notebooks, Synge refers to this lament as the cry of pain in which "the inner consciousness of the people seems to lay itself bare for an instant, and to reveal the mood of beings who feel their isolation in the face of a universe that wars upon them with wind and seas." *Riders to the Sea* palpitates with that wail of despair, whose rise and fall constitute the movement of the tragedy. There is little uncertainty as to the fate of Bartley, for we know at once that he has gone to join his brothers in death, but the tension is one of emotional suspense prepared with a skill surpassing the suggestive action of Maeterlinck's *Interior*. Synge hints at the approach of death by the interplay of seemingly irrelevant details, but their effectiveness is tremendously increased by the fact that each trifle contributes something to the naturalism of the *mise-en-scène*. There is not an action or a word but is doubly significant, first as part of the picture of manners, and secondly as a portent of the tragedy. The dramatist's hold on life is too profound to permit of his exercising mere literary ingenuity in the manipulation of symbols.

Before essaying his strength in the three acts of *The Well of the Saints*, Synge wrote a two-act comedy, *The Tinker's Wedding*, which belongs to the period of the two plays we have examined, although it was not published until 1907. Mr. John Masefield is authority for the statement that this was Synge's first attempt at dramatic writing, and its relative inferiority is evidence of that fact. The plot of *The Tinker's Wedding* is an elaboration of the anecdote, related in the author's notes on Wicklow, which told how two tinkers tried to have a priest bless their union, in return for a gallon can and a small sum of money, and how they afterwards pretended that the can had been damaged overnight by a kick from their ass. Synge might well have found in this, or his other Wicklow experiences, the substance of a short farce or a really good comedy, but the theme is not enough for the two acts of *The Tinker's Wedding*. The play follows too faithfully the main lines of the original story.

Sarah Casey and her companion, Michael Byrne, persuade the priest to marry them for "a bit of gold and a tin can." The first act is concerned with the ludicrous conversation between the priest and the tinkers, whose blandishments overcome his scruples against countenancing the flagrant irregularity of their lives and morals. But, as the scene closes, we see Michael's old mother going off with the tin can in search of refreshment, oblivious to its destined use in part payment of the marriage fee. When the curtain rises again, it is to show us the tinker family engaged in preparations for the consecration of their union, an event which excites old Mary Byrne to derision, and then to fear, when she finds that the can she exchanged for porter was to play so important a part. The astonishment of the prospective bride, when three empty bottles fall out of the packet in which the can had been wrapped is surpassed by the indignation of the priest. He re-

fuses to marry the couple for less than was stipulated,
and in a moment the three tinkers are against him —
Michael seizes and gags him, ties him up in a sack, and
threatens to throw him into the bog-hole; only by
promising not to inform the police does the priest eventually secure his freedom. With a Latin malediction
he terrifies his assailants, who run away, leaving him
master of the situation.

Seeing that such an inoffensive play as *In the Shadow
of the Glen* had aroused popular indignation, it is not
surprising that *The Tinker's Wedding* should not yet
have faced criticism in the Irish Theatre. The play
has never been performed in Ireland, and when produced in London, shortly after the author's death, it
was unfavorably received. Synge was accused of
atheism and anti-clericalism by those who condemned
the printed play, but the charge is untrue. He was
indulging rather that characteristic penchant for brutal,
sardonic humor, for which the irreverences of the
vagabond life of the roads supplied rich material.
His interest in tramps and outlaws may be traced to
his peculiar sense of humor whose satisfaction could
not be found in the orthodox existence of more sophisticated people. The note of *The Playboy of the Western
World* is easily perceptible in this first work for the
stage. Only the technical weaknesses of *The Tinker's
Wedding* differentiate it from Synge's later work.

As it happened, the dramatist had already revealed
the full quality of his talent when *The Tinker's Wedding*
was published. A few months earlier in the same year,
1907, *The Playboy of the Western World* had been issued

in book form, almost immediately after its riotous production at the Abbey Theatre. However, chronology
demands that we should consider Synge's first three-
act drama, *The Well of the Saints*, before giving our
attention to his masterpiece. It was one of the earliest
plays performed at the newly-opened Abbey Theatre
in 1905, and was published at the same time as the
first volume of that series to which the theatre gave its
name. Those who possess the fifteen issues of the
"Abbey Theatre Series" have in a convenient and
uniform edition the best that the Dramatic Revival
has produced. In *The Well of the Saints*, his fourth
play, Synge definitely proclaimed his control of the
dramatic medium by the ease with which he abandoned the one-act for the three-act form, the two acts
of *The Tinker's Wedding* having served to mark the
transition.

Doubtless because of the absence of any hint of
this play in the usual place, Synge's notebooks, much
misplaced energy has been expended in tracing it to
various sources, Chaucer and Maeterlinck, Zola and
Huysmans, Georges Clemenceau and Lord Lytton.
As will be seen, the theme is so universal in its appeal,
and so natural, that no such erudition is required to
explain Synge's choice. Martin and Mary Doul are
two old beggars, ugly and worn with hardships, whose
blindness has made them as unconscious of their own
defects as they are sensitive to the beauties of their
own world of imagination and intuition. To the village where they sit comes a saint who can work miracles
by means of the water from a holy well. He anoints

the eyes of the blind couple, whose sight is restored, with disastrous consequences to themselves and their neighbors. Gone are their illusions respecting their own persons, and instead we find them gifted with a dreadful candor which obliges them to utter all the unpleasant truths revealed by their clear-seeing eyes. Their friends are insulted, and they themselves are miserable at being deprived of those beautiful dreams with which blindness enabled them to transfigure material facts. They no longer hear "the birds and bees humming in every weed of the ditch, the swift flying things racing in the air." In the end, however, their eyes are darkened once more, and they rejoice in the imaginative existence of old. When the saint, on his return, tries to cure them again, Martin Doul knocks the holy water out of the friar's hand.

The Well of the Saints is the only occasion in Synge's career where he appears to express the traditional revolt of the Celtic mind against the despotism of fact. The refusal of the blind beggars to accept reality in place of the world of their dreams is an almost Yeatsian treatment of a situation which lends itself to his symbolical interpretation. Yeats, however, could not have injected the grim humor and realistic irony of Synge into a miracle story, though he would not have scrupled to run counter to religious prejudices, as the dramatist does in the *dénouement*, by causing Martin Doul to treat the saint with scant consideration. The gesture of the beggar in dashing the miraculous water to the ground has its parallel in the much disputed scene, in *The Countess Cathleen*, where Shemus stamps the shrine under foot. Those who have condemned Yeats as "un-Irish" on that account will doubtless find in *The Well of the Saints* a similar motive for applying the term to Synge. The play, nevertheless, is informed by the very spirit of the race, which finds its most obvious expression in the rhythmic prose of the idiom in which it is written. Its more subtle manifestations are defined by the relations of the two beggars to the external world of nature.

Having witnessed the culminating indecency of the campaign against *The Playboy of the Western World*, when the Irish Players were arrested at Philadelphia in 1912, the American public can have but a slight interest in the milder forms of a persecution which has long since expired in Ireland. The absurd story, moreover, has been so extensively related by critics of this too much discussed work, that recapitulation is both undesirable and unnecessary. It will be enough to say that notoriety immediately achieved for the author what his genius was but slowly acquiring, the attention of the serious public outside his own country. The noise made by his opponents gave his admirers in Ireland the opportunity of vindicating their belief in him, and, incidentally, of obtaining confirmation in their discernment, at the hands of educated criticism everywhere. Germany, as usual, had recognized the new genius in advance of his subsequent popularity abroad. Long before *The Playboy* was heard of, *The Well of the Saints* had been translated and was performed at Max Reinhardt's Theatre in Berlin, in 1906. But, generally speaking, Synge was the possession of a few until 1907, when his detractors forced him upon the notice of the reading public throughout the English-speaking world. It would be impossible to exaggerate the credit due to W. B. Yeats in this matter. A more timid mind would have shrunk from the odium of defying those who had, on the whole, befriended the work of the Dramatic Revival; a lesser personality would not have risked himself to forward the claims of the only writer whose fame could conflict with his own.

The now familiar narrative tells of the arrival of Christy Mahon in the "shebeen", or low saloon, of Michael James Flaherty, somewhere in County Mayo, and of the effect of his presence upon the inhabitants and frequenters of that resort. When Christy enters the cottage, Pegeen Mike, the daughter of the house, has just been left alone by her pusillanimous admirer and future husband, Shawn Keogh. Shawn would not stay unchaperoned with a young girl, so great is his deference to ecclesiastical authority. Pegeen Mike, disgusted at this supreme exhibition of timidity, is only too glad when the mysterious stranger comes upon the scene, and when it transpires that Christy has murdered his "da", she is the most interested of the group of villagers who crowd around to lionize the hero. The two are left alone and become increasingly attracted towards one another, the girl contrasting this brave and spirited young fellow with the miserable coward her parents have chosen for her — a typical specimen of a bad lot, whose defects are all the more manifest now that Christy is among them. All unite, except Shawn, in admiring the man for the qualities they themselves do not possess, and the womenfolk are jealous as to who shall carry off such a prize.

Pegeen Mike is determined that Christy shall marry her, and is never at a loss for expedients to discredit her rivals in his eyes. Not that this is necessary, for he is obviously infatuated by and flattered by the passion he has aroused in the village beauty. The amorous passages between Pegeen and Christy are instinct with a fine primitive poetry, admirably in harmony with the two personalities, and have been justly praised as being the most remarkable poetic writing in contemporary English. But the course of their love is not allowed to pass uninterruptedly. The playboy is induced to compete in the races being held in the village, and while he is away, his father arrives in search of the would-be parricide. Christy's blow had not killed, but only stunned, Old Mahon. His boasting is shown for what it is worth, and the halo of hero-worship falls from him, so far as Pegeen and the others are concerned. The subject of their recent admiration, however, has discovered new forces within himself. Instead of submitting to the blows of his father, as he used to do, Christy strikes him, in an attempt to consummate the crime for which he had previously been idolized. Then he learns that there is "a great gap between a gallous story and a dirty deed." Everybody turns against him when visible action is substituted for highly-colored narrative, and the two Mahons, father and son, are driven forth by universal hostility.

In one of his rare statements of literary doctrine, Synge declared the measure of serious drama to be "the degree in which it gives the nourishment, not very easy to define, on which our imagination lives." It is only by the application of that test that the manifold excellences of *The Playboy* may be discovered. Its imaginative strength, enhanced by its wonderful verbal qualities, constitutes the charm, for the language is the perfect complement of the emotional intensity of the dramatist's conception. Where the passion of his mood is exalted, as in the love passages of Christy and Pegeen Mike, speech rises to the level of the purest poetry. In the altercations between rivals, and the scenes of quarrel, the same medium becomes an instrument of human expression whose vigor and varied picturesqueness are paralleled only by the English of the Elizabethan era. This medium, now so universally admired, was the Anglo-Irish idiom of Gaelic Ireland. Not since Douglas Hyde's *Love Songs of Connacht* revealed the possibilities of peasant speech, nearly twenty years ago, had such effect been secured by the use of the idiom. Synge has admitted his share in the general debt to Hyde, whose experiments in Gaelicized English have shown the way to so many writers, notably to Lady Gregory, who is frequently credited with an originality not entirely hers. But where Hyde was a too cautious experimenter, and Lady Gregory a perceptible literary reporter, Synge showed himself a master. Guided by the example of the *Love Songs of Connacht*, he made a more intimate study from the living speech of the Western peasantry, and was able to say, in the preface to *The Playboy:* "I am glad to acknowledge how much I owe to the folk-imagination of these fine people."

The remarkable style of this play stands out when contrasted with the "Kiltartan English" of Lady Gregory's *Cuchulain of Muirthemne,* where the idiomatic phrasing has the air of a formula, cold and artificial, except where the inherent beauty of a phrase confers upon it some intrinsic merit. Synge does not mechanically reproduce what he has heard in the cottages; he molds the raw material, as it were, of peasant speech until it corresponds exactly to the impulse of his own imagination. Hence the delicate harmony of thought and phrase. He had so completely identified himself with the life of the people, and so thoroughly colored his vision with the Gaelic spirit of its original conception, that he could create where others reported. "In countries," he says, "where the imagination of the people, and the language they use, is rich and living, it is possible for a writer to be rich and copious in his words, and at the same time to give the reality, which is the root of all poetry, in a comprehensive and natural form." That sentence is at once an explanation and a characterization of Synge's work, especially when we recall his own words: "In Ireland, for a few years more, we have a popular imagination that is fiery and magnificent and tender; so that those of us who wish to write start with a chance that is not given to writers in places where the springtime of the local life is forgotten, and the harvest is a memory only."

Strange, indeed, is the perversity which insisted

upon a moral — or immoral — purpose in the writing
of *The Playboy*, and the other dramas which have
been condemned upon ethical grounds. Synge's attempts to reply to his censors have only added to the
preliminary confusion of thought upon which the
controversy was based. Instead of describing this
play as "an extravaganza" in the first wild moments of
popular indignation, and then withdrawing the term,
in order to engage upon a demonstration of the reality
of the facts alleged as libels, he would have done well
to keep silent. Failing that, he should have confined
himself to that explanation published shortly afterwards in the preface to *The Tinker's Wedding*: "The
drama, like the symphony, does not teach or prove
anything." As Synge complained, "in these days the
playhouse is too often stocked with the drugs of many
seedy problems", and we may be sure he had no desire
to add to the number. Unfortunately, by meeting
his critics on their own ground, he helped to inject an
alien element into all subsequent discussion of *The
Playboy*. Criticism is still preoccupied with the
problem of his "purpose" in writing that play. As if
one should speculate upon the libellous veracity of *Don
Quixote*, or examine *Tartarin de Tarascon* as a homily
upon the Eighth Commandment! Cervantes and
Synge both reconstructed imaginatively the moral
and psychological elements of a race, so that their
figures assume the significance of eternal human types.

The loss sustained by Irish literature through the
early death of Synge was sharply emphasized by the
posthumous publication of *Deirdre of the Sorrows*. This

unfinished tragedy was produced in 1910 at the Abbey
Theatre, and appeared in book form the same year.
In spite of the variously successful rehandling of this
classic theme by numerous predecessors, Synge's
version has such beauty and originality as could only
come from so powerful and independent a genius.   In
discussing the *Deirdre* of Yeats, we had occasion to
notice how he departed from the precedent of A. E.
by making the crisis in the Gaelic story his point of
departure, whereas Synge followed A. E. in dividing
the legend into three dramatic episodes.   At this point,
however, the resemblance between the two ceases.
Synge, with his innate sense of drama, and his profound
intuition of the Gaelic spirit, retold the tragedy of
Naisi and Deirdre in terms pulsating with heroic life.
His sure instinct for what is most national in the story
prompted him to transpose it into that key of contemporary nationality most attuned to the old Celtic origins
of the epic romance.   Deirdre is no longer a shadowy
personage of the heroic age, a legendary figure; she
is a wild, passionate woman, who struggles helplessly
against the fate which is to deprive her of life and love.

Although the play develops along the familiar lines
of the bardic tale, with only the strange character of
Owen as an innovation, there is an original and personal note in every line.   Whether it be Deirdre's
cry: "There are as many ways to wither love as there
are stars in a night of Samhain; but there is no way
to keep life, or love with it, a short space only.   It's
for that there's nothing lonesome like a love that is
watching out the time most lovers do be sleeping", or

Owen's warning: "Queens get old, Deirdre, with their white and long arms going from them, and their backs hooping. I tell you it's a poor thing to see a queen's nose reaching down to scrape her chin", — the imprint of Synge and of that Ireland nearest to the Celtic tradition is visible. Written while the author was dying, his end hastened by the strain of the *Playboy* controversy, *Deirdre* has all the sadness of Synge's own tragic conviction that "death is a poor untidy thing at best, though it's a queen that dies." The personal tragedy of the dramatist, and the intense reality of the characters drawn from a people allied by untamed nature to their prototypes of legend, combine to give this work an intensity unequaled by any other tragic writer. Unfinished as it is, *Deirdre* promises to be, if not Synge's masterpiece, the greatest modern version of the Gaelic classic. Not only is it humanly and dramatically more convincing than the plays of Yeats and A. E., but it contains such pure poetry as to make even the beautiful poem of the former seem poor in its lack of the passion inspiring the voice of Deirdre:

I have put away sorrow like a shoe that is worn out and muddy, for it is I who have had a life that will be envied by great companies. It was not by a low birth I made kings uneasy, and they sitting in the halls of Emain. It was not a low thing to be chosen by Conchubar who was wise, and Naisi had no match for bravery. It is not a small thing to be rid of grey hairs and the loosening of the teeth. It was the choice of lives we had in the clear woods, and in the grave we're safe surely.

Passages of this kind are frequent, and indicate what Synge's command of Anglo-Irish idiom would have meant for the future of the folk drama, had he lived long enough to carry out his intentions. For there can be little doubt but that he would have turned his attention to Irish legend, once he had realized his power to revivify and transfigure the epic material. It is known that he contemplated the breaking of new ground, and the play at which death interrupted him may be regarded as pointing the way of his proposed escape from the semi-realistic study of peasant life. Fundamentally *Deirdre* and *Riders to the Sea* are alike, in spite of the superficial air of realism which the setting of the latter confers upon it. Folk tragedy, even though the fable be classic, is the only term which accurately describes Synge's *Deirdre*, which is, therefore, an essential part of the author's work, not an exceptional experiment, as some have maintained. The creator of *The Playboy* was something more than an exponent of peasant drama, however much the more external aspects of his art have impressed his successors. They have adopted his form, but have failed, as a rule, to fill it with that subtle essence whereby Synge transformed reality until the real and the ideal were one. It is this imaginative re-creation which entitles him to a place amongst the great dramatists of the world's literature.

3

Padraic Colum

One, at least, of younger playwrights is free from the suspicion of having succumbed to the prestige conferred by Synge upon the peasant drama. Padraic Colum differs from his contemporaries by reason of his having given the measure of his originality before Synge had exerted any influence upon the work of the Irish Theatre. Although Colum's years place him among what is termed "the younger generation", his early beginning makes such a classification misleading. As previously stated, the *débuts* of Synge and Colum were contemporaneous, the latter's *Broken Soil* having followed *In the Shadow of the Glen* by a few weeks, in 1903. But if we take account of his activities prior to the organization of the Irish National Theatre Society, Colum's seniority is even more definitely established, not only as against the later dramatists with whom he is classed, but against Synge himself. Padraic Colum was one of the group with the brothers Fay which launched the movement whose succession to the task of the Literary Theatre has been related in an earlier chapter. About 1901 he came into contact with the embryonic association promoted by the Fays, and the interest of the experiment awoke in him the creative desire. The following year saw the publication of his first dramatic essays, *The Kingdom of the Young* and *The Saxon Shilling*. At the same time he actively participated in the enterprise of the circle by playing in A. E.'s *Deirdre*, at the inaugural performance of the National Dramatic Company as the successor of the Irish Literary Theatre. In short, Padraic Colum is one of the oldest workers in the movement which has given Ireland a National Theatre.

Like almost every Irish writer of to-day, Colum found in *The United Irishman* his first encouragement. That brave little journal of ideas, and its successor *Sinn Fein*, published the work of all who had anything to contribute to Irish culture, and in its files will be found the earliest, as well as the later, manifestations of many talents since known to fame. James Stephens wrote in its columns some of the most widely admired pages in his *Crock of Gold*, when only such an editor as Arthur Griffith had the discernment to print them. Drama and verse, particularly, met with his discriminating hospitality. Thanks to his initiative, such tentative writings as *Eoghan's Wife* and *The Foleys* were published while Colum was still feeling his way towards those realistic analyses of the peasant mind whose first important exposition was *Broken Soil*. For *Sinn Fein* the dramatist also wrote verse, in the company of Seumas O'Sullivan, James Stephens, Thomas MacDonagh, and a host of young poets, some of whose work was collected by A. E. for his little anthology, *New Songs* (1904). Encouraged by the reception of that book, several of these new singers issued their own poems, and amongst them Colum, whose *Wild Earth* appeared in 1907. This remarkable volume, through which breathed the essential spirit of folk poetry, was reissued later with additions, but the claims of the theatre were so to absorb the poet that he is only now promising us another book of verse.

After its production in 1903, *Broken Soil* was re-written, and did not make its appearance as a printed play until 1907, when it was entitled *The Fiddler's House*. This first play, like those that followed it, depends not at all upon the intricacies of external action. No other Irish dramatist dispenses so boldly with plots as Colum, who relies entirely upon the psychological interest of the situation presented by the grouping of character and motives. One is reminded of Ibsen, not the Ibsen of violent dénouements, as in *Hedda Gabler* or *Ghosts*, but the Ibsen of *A Doll's House*, which may well have suggested the second title of *Broken Soil*. Conn Hourican, the old fiddler, has the temperament of the artist, the restless longing for freedom and change, which are incompatible with the settled virtues of the peasant estate. His daughters are the victims of his improvidence, for only Maire understands him sufficiently to sympathize with his attitude towards life. Anne has the instinct of her class and race, which compels her to cling to the soil, and enables her to keep the affairs of the "bohemian" household in order.

The dramatist contents himself with setting Houri-can in this *milieu* of thrifty, responsible peasants, and by the intimate fidelity of the picture the contrast between the fiddler and his neighbors is dramatically exposed. The thoughts and cares of a rural community are depicted with the skill and knowledge which come only from a talent born and developed in similar

circumstances. When Conn Hourican finally obeys
the call of the roads, and sets off with Maire to live his
life as a strolling fiddler, we have obtained a glimpse
into the soul of a people. The characters of Colum's
drama are not the stereotyped figures of conventional
peasant melodrama, they are human beings drawn
straight from the heart of the Irish midlands. The
struggle whose climax closes the play has taken place
on a purely intellectual plane, as moving in its restraint
as the tragedy of Ibsen's Nora. Conn Hourican's
closing words are typical of the natural appeal of the
entire dialogue: "I'm leaving the land behind me,
too; but what's land after all against the music that
comes from far, strange places, when the night is on
the ground, and the bird in the grass is quiet?" Not
even the highly colored prose of Synge is more effective.

The "agrarian comedy" which preceded *The Fiddler's
House* was the author's first published work. *The
Land* appeared in 1905, as number three of that "Abbey
Theatre Series" of plays which opened with Synge's
Well of the Saints, and its literary merits correspond to
the high place there accorded to it. Only the two volumes of the series for which Synge was responsible can
claim superiority to this dramatization of the fundamental problem of peasant life, the call of the land. The
year of its production marked the closing scene of the
agrarian revolution in Ireland, for in 1905 the Irish
farmer was coming into possession of the land under
the terms of the Land Act of 1903, which definitely
established peasant proprietorship. Out of his deep
knowledge of rural conditions, Colum was able to

envisage the new prospect from a side not open to the casual observer.

The fatal attraction of the city is a commonplace amongst those interested in agricultural reform, but Ireland has to face the more serious competition of the United States. In *The Land* is shown how the youth and vigor of the countryside are drawn away by the lure of America. Murtagh Cosgar is a typical Irish farmer, with all the belief in parental authority and the claims of the family, characteristic of his race. No sacrifice is too great to preserve the land and the traditions of the house intact. His generation have fought and suffered for the ownership of the soil, but the emotion he would appeal to is dead in his son, Matt, who threatens to emigrate if his liberty is curtailed by parental interference. The old man submits, but he humbles in vain before a young generation, whose thoughts are fixed upon "the States." Matt, perhaps, would have felt something of the old peasant instinct towards the land, but his sweetheart, Ellen Douras, has been educated as a school-teacher, and her ambitions lie in a very different direction. America is everything to such intellectual *déracinés*, whose one desire is to escape to the centers of urban civilization. In the end Matt and Ellen go away, leaving the farm to the younger children, Cornelius Douras and Sally Cosgar, who are too stupid to take the risk of independent action. Old age and inefficiency are the recipients of the benefits for which generations vainly struggled and died.

The action of the play consists of a series of subtle

incidents which bring out the clash of two generations
of Irish peasants, the revolt of youth against the laws
of its elders. Rather than face the tyranny of the
family, the young people gladly seize upon the reported
advantages of life in America as an excuse for abandoning the land. They experience none of the joys of
victory, for they did not take part in the land wars of
which their chief recollection is the misery and suffering entailed. The tragedy is, therefore, in the fact
that now, when Ireland should be rebuilding its rural
society, the brains and energy of the peasantry have
been exported for industrial exploitation. *The Land*
is a poignant presentation of the question which forces
itself upon the attention of every thinking Irishman.
The answer is one which is engaging the best thought
of the country, and has found concrete expression
in the economic program of A. E. and his fellow-
workers outlined in *Co-operation and Nationality*.
That eloquent plea for reconstruction indicates the
nature of the reply to the query upon which the play
closes: "Do you ever think of the Irish nation that
is waiting all this time to be born?"

Elaborating a point raised in *The Land*, but viewing
it from an opposite angle, Padraic Colum wrote *Thomas
Muskerry* in 1910. The exigencies of a social system
in which the family unit replaces the industrial is a
theme which French writers have frequently studied,
but Colum is alone in his attempt to perform the same
service for Ireland. He does not, however, expand
the situations already noticed in the preceding play.
It is the father, not his children, who are made to suffer

from the abuse of family obligation: Thomas Muskerry, the master of Garrisowen Workhouse, is surrounded by two generations of relatives whose only wish is to make the utmost profit of their relationship with a man of some importance in a small country town. When his official retirement is hastened by the malpractice of a friend who has exploited his kindness, the family and dependents of Muskerry at once conspire to get rid of him, that they may the better establish themselves with his successor. This provincial Lear becomes the center of a series of sordid intrigues, which result in his utter destitution and abandonment at the hands of those whom he has benefited all the years of his active life. Muskerry dies on a pauper's bed in the institution of which he once was master, his only friend the blind piper, Myles Gorman, whom he considered in the days of his prosperity as a perfect example of a man without home or friends. An outcast and a vagabond, Myles is the only person who aids him, who remembers his goodness, and makes his last moments tolerable. Like another Père Goriot, Thomas Muskerry is killed by the selfish ingratitude of the family he has created.

These three plays are Colum's most important contribution to contemporary Irish drama. Each portrays some special aspect of rural life as seen by the peasant mind, and their common characteristic — which is significant — is the presence of conflict traceable to a family system involving the sacrifice of the individual. There is no attempt to formulate problems with a view to their solution, but only to present those situations which afford a dramatic insight into the workings of the folk nature. Padraic Colum was born in the Irish Midlands, and the drama of existence naturally projected itself upon his consciousness in terms of the peasantry whose world was his own. "The dramatist", he writes, "is concerned not primarily with the creation of character, but with the creation of situations . . . that will produce a powerful impression on an audience, for it is situation that makes the strongest appeal to our sympathies." With his own carefully restrained pictures before us, from which every adventitious or forced note is eliminated, it is easy to subscribe to this theory. His sobriety is, in its way, as impressive as the vivid fantasy of Synge.

Yet he has not confined himself exclusively to this naturalistic art. As far back as 1904 we find him working at that *Miracle of the Corn* which was published three years later in the little booklet *Studies* and was performed at the Abbey Theatre in 1908. In 1912 he published *The Destruction of the Hostel*, a belated return to his very youthful preoccupation with the heroic stories of Gaelic Ireland. Based upon Whitley Stokes's translation of *The Destruction of the House of Da Derga*, this fine little piece was well received when performed by the pupils of the late Padraic Pearse, at St. Enda's College, Dublin, in 1910. Since a tragic death has deprived Ireland of a notable figure in the history of our intellectual renaissance, that unique institution will doubtless disappear. Without the lofty idealism of Pearse, St. Enda's could not have become what it was. It is fortunate that the publication of Colum's play in the pages of *A Boy in Eirinn* (1913) should have preserved something to remind us of the literary side of an admirable educational innovation: the first experiment in genuinely Irish national education.

The grave and dignified prose of Colum's *The Destruction of the Hostel* promises much for the author should he turn to Gaelic literature for the material which he has heretofore found in his own experience. A determination to seek some new direction for his talent was revealed by the publication in 1912 of *The Desert*, just published in America under the title of *Mogu, the Wanderer*. This play, hastily issued to support a charge of plagiarism, has now been given the permanent revision which the dramatist had desired for it. Its main interest lies in the fact that the setting of this drama of Fate, full of the color of the East, gave the first clue to the author's new orientation. Since that time his imagination has been occupied with Byzantine history, and the romance of that vague Orient, which his compatriot, Lord Dunsany, has so splendidly divined.

Until we have been allowed to see the work of these experimental years, it would be premature to pass judgment upon the second manner of Padraic Colum, as exemplified in *The Desert*. If he can realize the unundeniable promise of that play, whose spectacular effectiveness easily surpasses the popular *Kismet* of Mr. Edward Knoblauch, his success would seem assured. It was the peculiar similarity of these two dramas which forced him to publish *The Desert*, in order to prove its long priority to a piece which had been justified on the ground of mere literary coincidence. Without denying him the right to express his fancy as it wills, one cannot help at the same time regretting, and preferring, the author of *The Land*, and *The Fiddler's House*. Murtagh Cosgar and Conn Hourican are not to be evoked by every dramatist, however gifted. Such figures could only be reconstructed by one whose roots in the soil are as deep as theirs. They are the true protagonists of the folk drama and could not have been conceived except in the spirit of the movement which Colum helped to initiate.

Unfortunately, like most of his early companions in that dramatic enterprise, including its originators the Fays, Padraic Colum has seen his work gradually neglected by the National Theatre. Coincidentally with the departure of the actors and playwrights to whose pioneering activities that institution owes its fame, his plays have disappeared from the current repertory of the Irish Players. Precedence has been given to those stereotyped farces and melodramas whose only claim to distinction is their Irish accent, and which are saved from utter banality by what still survives of the histrionic achievement of the brothers Fay. The newcomers have learnt the formulæ and can count upon popularity with those to whom the Irish Theatre is a species of eccentric show. They have adopted the external features of Colum's realism, as they have borrowed the superficial violences of Synge's verbal energy. With certain exceptions, to be noted subsequently, the later "Abbey playwrights" have contributed nothing personal to the development of the peasant play. J. M. Synge and Padraic Colum have between them prescribed the two modes of the *genre*, their complete dissimilarity being testimony to the original genius of each. At the cost of popular success, Colum has remained faithful to himself; he has withstood the temptation to melodramatize Synge.

CHAPTER VI

PEASANT COMEDY: LADY GREGORY AND WILLIAM BOYLE

1

Writing and Environment

WHILE the later imitative dramatists, under the influence of Synge, have specialized in scenes of violence, they have not been without models of another kind. Lady Gregory and William Boyle both established a reputation as comic writers at a comparatively early stage in the history of the Dramatic Revival, and, contrary to the experience of the majority of their colleagues at that time, neither has suffered from the advent of changed conditions. The exigencies of finance and the demands of essentially uncritical audiences, have modified to some extent the intentions of the founders of the Irish Theatre. But Lady Gregory and William Boyle have succeeded, not only in retaining the prominence denied to such pioneers as A. E. and Padraic Colum, but they have become the most popular playwrights of the new régime. Their work vies with that of the younger melodramatists of recent years, so that they may serve as a link between the pioneering era with which they were associated and the newcomers to whom the original organization is a vague tradition. Lady Gregory, it is true, wrote her maiden effort, *Twenty-five*, in 1903, when the Fays' group had just been reorganized as the Irish National Theatre Society, but her real success practically coincided with that of William Boyle, when the Abbey Theatre was opened to the public for the first season, in 1905. Ever since that date they have been more constantly before the public than other Irish dramatists.

Lady Gregory has been such an indefatigable worker on behalf of the Literary Revival in general, and of the Irish Theatre in particular, that it would be unjust to suggest the limitation of her rôle to the purveying of popular amusement. In a chapter of autobiography, *Our Irish Theatre* (1913), she has given an account of her participation in the movement which can leave no doubt as to the multiple nature of her services. Readers of that work will learn of considerable activities which could not have reached the knowledge of the outside world had she not disclosed them. So completely has she set forth the history of the Dramatic Revival, in its relation to herself, that nothing remains to be added by another hand. Socially, financially, and administratively, Lady Gregory has used her influence to foster the undertaking with which W. B. Yeats associated her, when A. E. had convinced him of the possibilities of W. G. Fay's company of players. Both her own statements and those of Yeats testify to the mutual advantage of their coöperation, and while this collaboration has been severely criticized on literary grounds, the devotion of Lady Gregory has never been questioned. It is possible to argue that the quality of Yeats's work has been diminished by the association of an art seriously at variance with his own; it cannot be denied that his activities for the advancement of the Irish Theatre have been strengthened and enlarged by the presence of a faithful collaborator.

Lady Gregory having herself placed on record the nature and extent of her share in the building up of the National Theatre, it is only necessary to refer to her general position in the world of Anglo-Irish letters. A brief consideration of her non-dramatic writings will enable us to turn to those specific contributions to contemporary Irish drama upon which the present estimate must be based. In addition to the volume of reminiscence already mentioned, Lady Gregory is the author of some half-dozen prose works, which are entitled to a higher place in contemporary Irish literature than any of her more popular plays: *Cuchulain of Muirthemne* (1902), *Poets and Dreamers* (1903), *Gods and Fighting Men* (1904), *A Book of Saints and Wonders* (1906). To these may be added, for completeness, two works of lesser importance, — *The Kiltartan Wonder Book* and *The Kiltartan History Book*, both published in 1910.

Cuchulain of Muirthemne and *Gods and Fighting Men* have been greeted with such extremes of praise and blame that their real merits and demerits have been obscured. The former volume is a retelling of the

Cuchulain legends; the latter performs the same service for the legends of the Fianna, as well as for the deities of Celtic mythology. In neither instance was Lady Gregory the initiator some have been led to believe. Numerous versions of these Gaelic stories had been made prior to the advent of the works in question, the most notable being the two volumes of Standish James O'Grady: *The History of Ireland: Heroic Period* (1878) and *The History of Ireland: Cuculain and his Contemporaries* (1880). This wonderful expression of an epic imagination kindled the enthusiasm of the poets, W. B. Yeats, A. E., and their friends from whom the Irish Literary Revival received its impulse. All the writers of their generation acknowledged O'Grady as the prophet who had led them into the rich fields of Gaelic poetry and tradition, and his fame in Ireland is all the more precious because it has never spread abroad. Few Irishmen will deny him the title of "Father of the Revival." The brilliant eloquence and ardent vision of O'Grady first brought the old bardic literature into circulation again, rescuing it from the laborious attention of translators and antiquarians.

Though he has not failed to voice his share in that prevailing admiration for O'Grady, W. B. Yeats has managed to convey the impression that, but for Lady Gregory, Gaelic legend and history would have remained in the obscurity of the learned societies. It is possible that some few of the younger generation in Ireland owe to her their first enthusiasm for the heroic tales, but even the youngest poets have learned much from O'Grady. The original character of Lady Gregory's versions lies rather in their composition and style. She has taken all the available texts, and by a process of coördination and elimination has welded them into a homogeneous and consecutive narrative. At the same time she has employed peasant idiom, in order to evoke the atmosphere in which the legendary lore of Gaelic Ireland is still living, in the cottages of the West, where the old traditions are preserved. Both these innovations have been severely criticized. On the one hand, it is argued that the original text is distorted by this arbitrary method of collation, on the other, that the monotony and artificiality of the idiomatic style deprive the old epics of their virile nobility. This criticism would be more forcible, perhaps, if Lady Gregory were the sole source to which the reader could turn for information. But translations of varying degrees of accuracy are available, from the scholarly publications of the Irish Texts Society, — *The Cuchullin Saga* of Eleanor Hull, for example, — to the vivid historical reconstructions of O'Grady. There can be no question as to the popular value of such works as Lady Gregory's, and it is with the general public in mind that one can indorse the laudatory comments of W. B. Yeats, who holds *Cuchulain of Muirthemne* and its companion volume to be the Irish equivalent of Malory's *Morte d'Arthur*.

Poets and Dreamers, like *A Book of Saints and Wonders*, has an interest of a documentary rather than a literary nature. Both consist largely of brief fragments and anecdotes which are illustrative of the folk imagination, as the idiom is an illustration of folk speech. Reading them, one understands where Lady Gregory amassed that wealth of verbal humor upon which her comedies rely for their effect. The first-mentioned book is valuable for its sympathetic essay on the poetry of Douglas Hyde, who originated the idiomatic method so greatly extended by Synge and Lady Gregory. It also contains translations of his verse and of four plays from the Gaelic. Lady Gregory has translated a number of Hyde's dramatic pieces, thereby strengthening her skill in the adaptation of Gaelicized English to the needs of literature. Her Kiltartan books are exercises of a similar kind, being simple narratives of history and folklore told in what has now become known as "Kiltartanese", the speech of the country people in the district of Kiltartan, near the author's home in County Galway. This dialect has become familiar through its constant employment by Lady Gregory in the plays she has written for the Irish Theatre. Not the least successful, and certainly the most original, occasion of its use was in those remarkable translations of *Le Médecin malgré lui*, *Les Fourberies de Scapin*, and *l'Avare*, which were performed at the Abbey Theatre during its first years, and appeared in 1910 as *The Kiltartan Molière*.

2

The Comedies of Lady Gregory

With the exception of *The Unicorn from the Stars*, which has already been mentioned amongst the works

of W. B. Yeats, and *Twenty-five*, her first effort at
dramatic writing, the plays of Lady Gregory have
been collected into five volumes: *Seven Short Plays*
(1909), *The Image* (1910), *New Comedies* (1913), and
two collections of *Irish Folk History Plays* (1912). Of
all these, the first-mentioned contains her best and
most characteristic work, including, as it does, those
inimitable one-act farces which have never been long
absent from the stage of the Abbey Theatre since its
inception.   Strange to say, the author's first contribution to the repertory of the Irish Players was a serious
drama, *Twenty-five*, which has never been published
since its performance in 1903.   The following year Lady
Gregory wrote *Spreading the News*, the forerunner of
those numerous little comedies with which her name
is now associated.   In rapid succession came *Hyacinth
Halvey*, *The Jackdaw*, *The Rising of the Moon*, and
The Poorhouse, and in 1907 three of her plays were
issued in the Abbey Theatre Series, under the title,
Spreading the News and other comedies.   When the
larger volume, *Seven Short Plays*, was published, *The
Poorhouse* had been rewritten as *The Workhouse Ward,*
and two pieces of a very different character were
added, *The Gaol Gate* and *The Travelling Man*.

The substance of these typical plays is too slight
to bear summary.   The usual starting point is some
ridiculous misconception, which enables the characters
to react grotesquely, as in *The Jackdaw*, where a mis-
understanding leads to an absurd competition amongst
the villagers, who believe that a large sum of money
will be paid to them for every jackdaw they capture.

In *Spreading the News* similar fun is derived from the distortion of an innocent remark by the credulous gossips of a village, which is thrown into a state of comic upheaval by the imaginary fears of its inhabitants. There is more genuine satire in *The Workhouse Ward*, with its humorous picture of two old paupers whose quarrels never cease until they are at the point of being separated. Then they sink their animosities and will not be parted. Since only one of them can be released, they prefer to remain together, but as the curtain falls, they are seen renewing in the most violent fashion their habitual war of words. *The Rising of the Moon* is an even better comedy of Irish nature : with its whimsical story of a policeman's struggle between his official duties and his national and personal sympathy for the rebel whom it is his business to arrest. The development of the incidents which finally persuade him to let his prisoner escape is very skilful. Illustrative of another aspect of the same question is *The Gaol Gate*, one of Lady Gregory's finest works. Here the tragedy is that of a mother who comes to the prison where her son is held for a political offense. Grieved as she is at his loss, her grief is embittered by the belief that he has turned informer to escape death. When she learns that he has paid the extreme penalty rather than betray his friends, her *caoin* is one of mingled lament and joy at the thought of his patriotic faith.

In *New Comedies*, Lady Gregory has collected her more recent one-act plays, *The Bogie Men*, *The Full Moon*, *Coats*, *Damer's Gold*, and *McDonough's Wife*.

None of these equals the earlier comedies; the original verve and zest have made way for a certain mechanical effect which must be attributed to excessive exploitation of the same material. That this material is thin would seem to be indicated by the author's having had recourse to the device of resuscitating the characters of previous works. Amusing as Hyacinth Halvey was in the play of that name, he ceases to be so when regalvanized in *The Full Moon*, a play utterly devoid of good humor. There is a noticeable tendency in the later comic work of Lady Gregory towards the use of the most hackneyed *ficelles* of the conventional farce. *Coats* is of the species of curtain-raiser familiar to all patrons of vaudeville.

On the other hand, *The Image*, the writer's most ambitious comedy, was a promising departure from the stereotyped farce. Its three acts center about a motive which has been developed with greater success by George Birmingham in *General John Regan*, — both plays having been derived from a suggestion of the poet, A. E. Those who have seen the latter play will be interested in comparing the treatment of an identical theme by two authors who have specialized in the humors of Irish life. As Lady Gregory works out the idea, that of honoring a wholly imaginary great man, the theme is radically modified, whereas George Birmingham confines his attention to the superficial comedy of such a situation. She describes how unexpected wealth comes in the shape of two whales to a poor village in the west of Ireland. The great fish are lying on the shore, and the protagonists of the play

are speculating as to what they will do with their share
of the proceeds when the oil is sold. The priest pro-
poses that the money be spent for the good of the village, so it is decided to erect a statue to a certain Hugh
O'Lorrha, for reasons whose exposition is the occasion
of excellent satire. Days pass in quarreling and de-
bating about the expenditure of the money, until it is
discovered that all the oil has been drawn from the
blubber of one whale by the men of a neighboring community, while the other has been carried out to sea
by the high tide. There is an undercurrent of satirical
criticism in *The Image* which is absent from the rollick-
ing good humor of *General John Regan*, but while the
latter realizes its author's more modest intentions, the
former just fails to be convincing.

3

The Plays of Folk History

The most original, if the least successful, part of
Lady Gregory's dramatic writings will be found in the
six *Folk-History Plays*, especially the three "tragic
comedies", *The Canavans*, *The White Cockade*, and *The
Deliverer*. The three tragedies, *Grania*, *Kincora*, and
Devorgilla, are not such innovations in the treatment of
legendary or historical themes. They are but sys-
tematic attempts to do what Synge achieved, in *Deirdre
of the Sorrows*, by the instinct of genius : to translate the
subjects of classical tragedy into terms of folk drama.
Kincora, for example, the earliest of these tragedies,
deals with a situation out of Irish history. Brian, King

of Munster, receives Malachi, the High King of Ireland, at his royal house at Kincora, that they may try
to arrange terms of peace in a mutually satisfactory
manner. The two chieftains who are opposed to the
arrangement, by which Malachi and Brian arrogate
to themselves dominion over the North and South
respectively, are afterwards defeated at the battle of
Glenmama. The High King would condemn Sitric
and Maelmora to death, but, at the instance of Queen
Gormleith, whose son and brother are thus about to
die, Brian champions the two offenders. Subsequently
he overcomes Malachi, and receives as part of his victory the hand of Gormleith, for "the Queen of Tara
must not lose the crown of Tara." As Malachi, however, foresaw, she could not exist without perpetual
strife, being a captured Dane, without any feeling of
pride in the country forced upon her. With her son,
Sitric, Gormleith joins forces with the Danish invasion
which Brian defeats at the battle of Clontarf, only to
be killed himself in the hour of victory, his spirit crushed
by the treacherous conduct of the Queen.

The melodramatic incoherence of *Kincora* was doubtless due in some measure to the fact that it was the
author's first attempt at historical reconstruction. It
has been drastically revised since its original publication and production in 1905, the prologue, and two
scenes in the third act having been omitted when it
was revived in 1909. But the play of three acts does
not seem to be within the scope of Lady Gregory's
talent, as we noticed in the case of *The Image*. The
"one-acter" shows her, as a rule, at her best, as was

demonstrated when *Devorgilla,* the second of her folk-history tragedies, was produced in 1907. Foreign critics have not been able to sense the appeal of this essentially national episode. Devorgilla is the old Queen of Breffny who was responsible, in the days of her youth, for bringing the English into Ireland. She is living a secluded and almost anonymous existence at the Abbey of Mellifont, but the chance singing of a passing minstrel brings before her the tale of the havoc wrought by her former misdeeds. The unconscious offender is driven into the English camp by Devorgilla's servant, Flann, whose life is taken by the enemies of his country. The bereaved widow, in mourning her husband's death, reveals the identity of the old Queen to the assembled people, to whose sports Devorgilla had been invited as prize-giver. As soon as they know who she is, they return contemptuously the trophies she has distributed, and the Queen submits to the insult, for she recognizes the justice in the "swift, unflinching, terrible judgment of the young." As played by Miss Sara Allgood, the part of Devorgilla was informed by all the tragic pathos of a life conscious of its responsibility for unutterable woe.

By far the best of Lady Gregory's experiments in serious folk drama is her as yet unacted *Grania,* which alone can be compared with Synge's consummate achievement in this *genre.* The love story of Diarmuid and Grania is to the Fenian cycle of Irish legend what that of Naisi and Deirdre is to the earlier Ossianic cycle, but it has exercised no corresponding fascination upon the poets. With the exception of that curious

play in which Moore and Yeats collaborated for the
Irish Literary Theatre in 1901, this work of Lady
Gregory's is the only dramatization of the subject which
the Revival has seen. Grania is to marry Finn of
Almhuin, but she prefers the youthful Diarmuid, with
whom she flees into the wilderness, where they wander
for seven years. Faithful to his pledge, Diarmuid
refuses to become the lover of Grania, but, finally,
circumstances force him to forget his vow, and for a
brief week the couple live as man and wife. Grania,
however, discovers that his resistance constituted
Diarmuid's chief charm, and, once he has surrendered,
her thoughts turn to other conquests. The lovers
are about to quarrel when Finn arrives, in the guise
of a beggar, to reproach Diarmuid with treachery.
Touched with remorse, the young warrior rushes forth
to fight for his master, and is slain. Whereupon Grania
devotes her attentions to Finn, transferring her way-
ward affection from youth to old age. This she could
do for the reason that her feminine pride had keenly
suffered from that faithfulness to Finn, which so long
kept Diarmuid out of her power. That, at least, is
Lady Gregory's interpretation of a character whose
psychology presented itself to George Moore in less
subtle terms — terms which brought upon the collaborators the accusation of having transformed a beautiful legend into "the plot of an average French
novel."

The influence of Synge is evident in *Grania*, which
rises above the fairly commonplace level of its companion plays precisely in proportion as it emulates

his manner. His rhythms are in such speeches as: "But you and I could have changed the world entirely, and put a curb upon the springtide, and bound the seven elements with our strength," and "It was at that time he had done with deceit and he showed where his thought was, and had no word at all for me that left the whole world for his sake, and that went wearing out my youth, pushing here and there as far as the course of the stars of Heaven", or "my love that was allotted and foreshadowed before the making of the world will drag you in spite of yourself, as the moon above drags the waves, and they grumbling through the pebbles as they come, and making their own little moaning of discontent." Yet, one cannot compare the eloquent beauty of Synge's poetic idiom with these somewhat forced effects, without feeling that the latter are echoes rather than the expression of an original sense of verbal music.

If we pass over the misplaced ingenuity of *The Deliverer*, in which allegory serves to illustrate the fate of such patriots as Parnell, there remain two tragi-comedies to whose unique character allusion has already been made. Just as Yeats approached the heroic age for the poetic farce of *The Green Helmet*, Lady Gregory brings out the comic aspect of certain phases of Irish history hitherto regarded with tragic seriousness. *The Canavans* (1906) is an extravaganza of general, rather than particular import, in which are burlesqued the difficulties of the miller, Canavan, who tries to prove himself a loyal subject of Queen Elizabeth. The supposed arrival of the Queen in

Ireland supplies material for farcical comedy differing
in nothing, except its historical setting, from the
author's farces of contemporary peasant life. On the
other hand, precise and bitter satire is the basis of
The White Cockade, which is easily first in order of
merit, as it was the first to be produced, of Lady
Gregory's historical comedies. It was played at the
Abbey Theatre a year earlier than *The Canavans*, and
was her second play to appear in book form. *Kincora*
and *The White Cockade* were respectively volumes II and
VIII of the Abbey Theatre Series, and were issued
during 1905, the first year of its publication.

The scene is laid at Duncannon, where King James
the Second retreated after the Battle of the Boyne.
The cowardly King has planned to escape on a French
ship, abandoning the brave Sarsfield and the men who
fought with him against William of Orange. His
craven dependence upon Sarsfield is not at end, however, for when James inadvertently comes upon a band
of Williamites in an inn where he takes refuge, it
is the general who saves him, by impersonating the
King, and even winning over the enemy to his side.
Unmoved by this further proof of bravery and loyalty,
James pursues his determination to flee from his followers, and induces some French sailors to take him
on board concealed in a barrel. Again he falls into
the hands of his enemies, for the soldiers of William
open this very cask to quench their thirst, but Sarsfield persuades them to let so miserable a creature go
free. As he broods over the betrayal of Ireland's faith
by King James, Sarsfield pulls out the feathers of his

cockade, counting each one as an attribute of the
monarch, after the well-known game of childhood,
until the last feather falls at the word "thief." James
is neither king nor knave, soldier nor sailor, tinker nor
beggar man ; he is the thief, who has robbed the Irish
people of their honor. Nevertheless, the general will
continue to fight for those ignominiously forsaken by
the King. Equipped with a fresh cockade, picked up
from the scattered emblems thrown away by the dis-
illusioned soldiers of James, Patrick Sarsfield sets out
to champion the lost cause.

Such a treatment of one of the most delicate and
dangerous subjects in Irish history indicates that Lady
Gregory is able to bring considerable impartiality to
the portrayal of national subjects. The dramatists
of the Irish Theatre have broken with the tradition
which demanded the patriotic idealizations of melodrama from all who essayed to dramatize the history
of Ireland's struggle for freedom. We shall have
occasion to cite instances of this tendency in the
next chapter. While crediting the author of *Grania*
and *The White Cockade* with the originality of these
experiments in folk history, we must not overlook the
literary quality of her work. From that point of view
it is easier to approve of her intentions than to praise
their realization. What has been said of *Grania* is
true of folk-history plays as a whole. Their relation
to Synge is their degree of excellence, whether they
be derivative or not. *The Canavans* preceded *The
Playboy*, yet the leading motive is the same ; *Grania*
followed *Deirdre of the Sorrows* and bears traces of its

influence. Both dramatists studied the same people, and may well have reached an identity of mood because of this common origin of their dramatic world. But precisely this community of material involves contrasts which give precedence to Synge, and make us more than usually sensible of Lady Gregory's weaknesses.

Her own judgment in this matter is sound. Speaking of the circumstances which led her to essay historical drama instead of peasant comedy she says: "Perhaps I ought to have written nothing but these short comedies, but desire for experiment is like fire in the blood." Lady Gregory is remembered as the author of *The Workhouse Ward* and *The Gaol Gate* rather than as the experimental writer of folk tragedies and tragi-comedies. Within the limitations of one short act she can obtain effects of humor and pathos, denied to her longer plays, which have secured her place in the affection of all who are interested in the Irish Theatre. An analysis of the programs of the Abbey Theatre will reveal the phenomenal popularity of Lady Gregory, whose one-act comedies are performed twice and three times as often as those of any other playwright. There is something excessive in this complacent bidding for purely popular favor. In the season of 1912, for example, sixteen performances of *The Rising of the Moon* were given, as against three of *The Playboy*, while *Thomas Muskerry* was not presented even half as often as *The Workhouse Ward*. The latter was surpassed, in its turn, by the ineffable *Coats*, which was produced on no less than twelve occasions during a season of thirty plays. Granting the charm of such whimsical drolleries of speech and situation as Lady Gregory originally conceived, it is impossible to reconcile them with the claims of literary drama. Her predominant position in the repertory of the Irish Theatre hardly corresponds to what is permanent in her contribution to Irish literature.

4

The Comedies of William Boyle

Akin to that of Lady Gregory is the work of William Boyle, whose three and four-act comedies are the counterpart of her short farces, in their successful and constant appeal to popular audiences. It was not until 1905, when the Abbey Theatre was opened, that Boyle's name was associated with the Dramatic Movement. He was known as a writer of verse and short stories for the newspapers, and had published a collection of peasant studies of the County Louth, a *Kish of Brogues*, in 1899. His published plays are four in number, and were published and produced as follows: *The Building Fund* (1905), *The Eloquent Dempsey* (1906), *The Mineral Workers* (1906), and *Family Failing* (1912). In 1907 the author seceded from the Irish Theatre as a protest against Synge, whose *Playboy* did not meet with his approval. He eventually returned to give his *Family Failing*, and has since enjoyed the satisfaction of seeing three or four performances of that play in each season to one of Synge's masterpiece.

The Building Fund is the only work which calls for more than passing comment. It was written out of that knowledge of the Louth peasantry which was evident in the author long before he was attracted to the theatre by the first London visit of the Irish Players. While *The Eloquent Dempsey* and *Family Failing* are commonplace caricature, farcical to an extreme only found in a few of Lady Gregory's latest comedies, *The Building Fund* is a sincere picture of rural manners. It relates how Mrs. Grogan, a grasping old woman, succeeds in defeating her equally selfish son and granddaughter, on the pretext of performing an act of charity. When two farmers call to ask for her contribution to the building fund of the new church, she and her son drive them away empty-handed. But she has conceived a plan whereby the greedy calculations of Shan and Sheila will come to nought, even when her much-wished-for death takes place. When the farmers return on another occasion, she contributes to their collection by making a will leaving her money to the church. The plot is of the slightest, yet, so excellent is the characterization of the various types, and so skillfully is the dialogue woven, that the play holds the audience and the reader alike.

Technically the later plays are perhaps more perfect in their conformity to the accepted conventions of the "well-written" comedy. Surprises and stage effects are plentiful in the comedy of Jeremiah Dempsey, the opportunist politician whose eloquence betrays him, and in *The Mineral Workers*, with its account of the difficulties experienced by an Irish-American when he tries to arouse the energies and enterprise of a community whose soil is rich in mineral qualities. Yet neither can be compared to that first play through which one feels the throb of real life, and hears the voices of authentic human beings. The variety of characters and motives is beyond the dramatist's control in *The Mineral Workers,* while the absence of every dramatic element renders *Family Failing* as tiresome as its artificiality is incredible. The degradation of a powerful theme was never more striking than in this dull farce, which might have been a great comedy. In the hands of a writer who could exploit the dramatic quality of the theme, — the demoralizing effect of laziness and improvidence upon all who are subjected to their influence, — a fine play would have resulted. As it is we must conclude that William Boyle had given his best when the early enthusiasm of the Fay's organization stirred him to write *The Building Fund.*

He has been encouraged to cater for the facile success of immediate popularity, which he and Lady Gregory alone, of all the earlier dramatists, share between them. The effect has been a gradual deterioration in the quality of the plays presented at the Abbey Theatre, accompanied by a corresponding decline in the nature of the audiences. Instead of educating public taste, everything is done to encourage people who come to be amused by an unusual spectacle, to get a change from the too familiar pleasures of the English drawing-room play and the musical comedies, which are the main part of England's contribution to the Irish stage. Comic effects are secured by decking out imbeciles and brutes in the shreds and tatters of peasant speech, and the superficial violence of melodrama replaces the drama of character, which can only come from an inner life. There are still new dramatists, however, worthy of the best traditions of the National Theatre, as we shall see in the following chapter.

CHAPTER VII

LATER PLAYWRIGHTS

THE reproaches made by competent critics against certain recent tendencies of the National Theatre are based mainly upon two points, the comparative or total neglect of the more serious writers, and the too frequent production of the same plays, most of which have only the most ephemeral interest. It seemed as if the dramatists subsequent to 1907, the year of *The Playboy*, were to enjoy prominence not only at the expense of their predecessors, but also to the detriment of the artistic standards and traditions of the Dramatic Movement. In 1908 the Abbey Theatre had become notorious and famous, and the date may be said to have marked the advent of a third phase in the history of the Revival. *Samhain*, the organ of the Theatre, ceased to appear, and, by a strange coincidence, the principles and theories for which it stood became perceptibly less noticeable in the work of the new playwrights.

At the same time the withdrawal of Miss Horniman's subsidy made it difficult to proceed with that disregard for financial considerations which had been a source of much strength. Dramatists were given preference when they combined a sufficient appearance of artistic worth with the qualifications likely to react favorably upon the receipts. Nevertheless, as a result of considerable criticism and controversy in the Irish press, a compromise was reached. New plays were produced instead of the eternal comedies of Lady Gregory and William Boyle, and the melodramas of W. F. Casey, Lennox Robinson, and T. C. Murray made way for the works of men who had prior claims upon the attention of the public. The most remarkable writer thus saved from the oblivion which threatened him was George Fitzmaurice, whose plays were restored to the repertory of the Abbey Theatre a couple of years ago.

1

George Fitzmaurice

When *The Country Dressmaker* was revived in 1912, the author had faded almost completely from the memory of all but the few who recognized the promise of the young dramatist when that play introduced him in 1907. In 1908 George Fitzmaurice followed up his first contribution with a second of slighter texture, *The Pie-dish*. This curious little piece in one act, which failed to secure the sympathies of an audience already in search of digestive amusement, was soon forgotten on the accession of the new régime of imitative peasant playwrights. It is not surprising, therefore, that he should have waited for seven years before publishing his first play. Meanwhile, in spite of discouragement, Fitzmaurice had not been idle. In 1914

The Country Dressmaker had scarcely appeared, when it was supplemented by a volume entitled *Five Plays*, containing *The Moonlighter*, *The Magic Glasses*, and *The Dandy Dolls*, as well as the two plays already mentioned.

As is the case in the best of our folk drama, *The Country Dressmaker* is contrived out of the simplest elements. Julia Shea, the sentimental dressmaker, has remained faithful through many years to Pats Connor, who went off to the United States to make his fortune. Julia is addicted to romantic fiction and jealously nurses her love for the absent Pats, whom she endows with all the virtues of the novelette hero. One day Connor arrives unexpectedly and learns, while asking for news of the old folk, how the dressmaker has waited for him. His astonishment is great, for he has never communicated with her, and was married in America without a thought for what he remembered as a boy and girl love affair. Then he is told how Julia has been fooled into believing that he loves her by hearing passages read out from letters which were never written. Connor is touched by this cruel trick and tries to live up to the part attributed to him, but not very successfully, as it seems to the romantic mind of Julia, who contrasts his changed appearance with the conditions portrayed in the novels. The intrigues of a neighbor with marriageable daughters almost ruin the prospects of Julia's marriage, but in the end she is reconciled to Pats Connor, and turns, with great natural dignity, from the imaginary world of fiction to accept the realities of everyday life.

The play is packed with observation, and is brilliantly written, in an idiom rich with quaint terms and delectable words, which, nevertheless, differs fundamentally from the stereotyped "Kiltartanese" and its variants, to which so many writers have abandoned themselves. Here and there one is shocked by gross caricature, whose defects are emphasized by the faithful characterization of most of the figures in this perfect comedy of rural manners. Seldom has a first play shown such qualities of style and dramatic technique as *The Country Dressmaker*. The great development of the author's talent during the seven years which followed it did not surprise those who read *Five Plays* with a precise impression of Fitzmaurice's début. For *The Pie-dish* gave a hint of that imaginative power which we shall find to be the complement of the author's folk-realism. It dealt with the culminating moment in the struggle of an old man to obtain the satisfaction of his artistic instinct. Leum Donoghue has worked for years molding a pie-dish, a work in which the artist that is in him has found refuge from the incomprehension of his humble surroundings. He is dying, and in fitful bursts of energy and consciousness demands to be allowed to finish his task. His children are more concerned to have the priest administer the last sacraments, but Leum craves only time to achieve his little masterpiece. The priest appeals to him in vain to prepare for the end, the artist refuses to surrender, and appeals to the devil, in default of God, to grant him the necessary respite. He will sell his soul for time in which to complete the pie-dish, and as he dies, with the blasphemy on his lips, his work falls from his hand and is shattered. Father Troy pronounces him damned, but his children are convinced that the idealism of their father will meet with a better fate.

The Moonlighter is a more conventional type of play, and belongs to the same order as *The Country Dressmaker*, although its four acts are given over to tragedy rather than to comedy. As the title itself explains, the scene takes place during the troubled times of the agrarian revolution in Ireland. Peter Guerin is a splendid type of the old Fenian, whose ardor is strong, though years have taught him prudence and limited his activity. The district is full of young fellows who are arming and training against the day when they must fight for their rights and liberties. Eugene, his son, is one of the most enthusiastic of the hotheads, whose constant parade of nationality arouses the skepticism of Guerin. The father opposes his son's ambition to join in a moonlighting expedition against a neighboring farmer, and Eugene leaves home in defiance of Guerin's wishes. When he next comes upon the scene, he has been away in the city for a year, having fled at the last moment before the consequences of his desire to be a moonlighter. Meanwhile outrages have been taking place, and his erstwhile companions are in conflict with the police. Eugene, however, has lost his sympathy with the methods of physical violence; all the claptrap which he used to utter for the benefit of his father has evaporated. The real man is revealed a craven timeserver, without a spark of patriotic energy. When the moonlighters are pursued by the police, and one comes like a hunted animal to Guerin's house, Eugene has nothing but cautious advice to offer. The old Fenian's spirit, however, is aroused, he rushes out to face the rifles of the police in an attempt to aid a young friend, whose courage has convinced Guerin that all the young men are not like Eugene, and that the soul of revolt still lives in a new generation. He is killed with the others, and Eugene is left to meet the contempt of his friend and family.

Some of the typical violence of the new conventional peasant melodrama mars *The Moonlighter*, but Fitzmaurice is too good a craftsman to succumb to mere formulæ. He has made a penetrating study of the conditions which breed violence in peasant Ireland, and he depicts the knaves and braggarts with the same care as the patriotic idealists. Peter Guerin is a remarkable characterization, and though he necessarily has all the sympathy of an Irish audience, he must be recognized as a fine psychological portrait, equaled, perhaps, by Eugene. The play shows a distinct advance upon *The Country Dressmaker* in the contrivance and the manifestations of incident. In spite of its greater length, the interest is sustained to a moving climax.

Together with an increasing technical skill, Fitzmaurice shows an ever greater command of picturesque and forcible idiom, which finds its maximum expression in *The Magic Glasses* and *The Dandy Dolls*. These two plays are in one act, and have neither the style nor the substance which would repay an attempt to summarize them. The former piece is a realistic fantasy, which relates to the world in which we live, but the latter is an exercise of pure fancy, situated beyond the limitations of human experience. The "magic glasses", which have bemused Jaymony Shanahan, belong to the same order as the "dandy dolls" made by Roger Carmody, and both plays are the narrative of a wildly grotesque struggle against the forces of the supernatural. Whereas the witch-doctor who professes to cure Jaymony is a humorous idealization of the eternal charlatan, the Grey Man and Hag's Son who steal the windpipes from the throats of Carmody's dolls are creatures of the same race as the Trolls of Ibsen. There is also a suggestion of the Norwegian poet in *The Magic Glasses*, where the loft to which Jaymony retires in order to enjoy the fairy music reminds us of the garret in *The Wild Duck*, within whose shelter the old grandfather was transported to a world of the imagination. Similarly Shanahan is lured by the magic glasses, which bring him the oblivion of humdrum affairs which he desires.

In the domain of pure fantasy George Fitzmaurice has only one rival, Lord Dunsany, while in the vigor and exuberance of his peasant speech he is surpassed by Synge, but unequaled by any other of the Irish dramatists. There is none of the poetry of Synge's language in Fitzmaurice's plays, but there is the same wealth of virile and vivid phrasing, in which every speech is "as fully flavoured as a nut or apple", to quote the preface to *The Playboy*. The "joyless and pallid words", which Synge condemned, find no place in what Fitzmaurice has written, though he never uses an expression traceable to any of his predecessors. The Anglo-Irish idiom as he employs it offers no analogies either with Hyde and Synge or Lady Gregory, beyond the fact of their common source in Gaelic. He has made of peasant speech an original creation which, if not the potent instrument of Synge, is measurably finer than the monotonous "Kiltartanese" and its minor variants, in vogue with the later playwrights. George Fitzmaurice has, therefore, imagination and style of a sufficiently personal quality to give him rank as the greatest folk-dramatist since the death of J. M. Synge, and the practical withdrawal of Colum's plays from the current repertory of the Abbey Theatre.

2

Seumas O'Kelly

If George Fitzmaurice were offered as an example of a writer first encouraged, and then neglected, by the directors of the National Theatre, Seumas O'Kelly is an instance of the contrary, his work having been recognized elsewhere before it found acceptance in that quarter. His first four plays, *The Matchmakers*, *The Stranger*, *The Shuiler's Child*, and *The Homecoming* were all produced by an amateur organization called "The Theatre of Ireland" before the directors of the Abbey Theatre realized his merits. *The Matchmakers* appeared in book form in 1908, and was reissued in 1912, with the two other "one-acters", under the title, *Three Plays*. Meanwhile *The Shuiler's Child* had been published in 1909, and the following year it became part of the repertory of the Irish Players, eighteen months after its first production. It was for some years the only work of Seumas O'Kelly played by them, until he wrote *The Bribe*, which they performed in 1913. One cannot refrain from wondering why none of his shorter pieces has been taken to relieve the monotony of repeated performances of the same curtain-raisers, necessitated by the requirements of the Abbey Theatre programs. Although they do not call for detailed exposition, *The Stranger* and *The Homecoming* are well entitled to consideration, dealing, as they do, with situations whose appeal to Irish audiences is certain.

It is strange that a work of such merit as *The Shuiler's Child* should so long escape the attention of W. B. Yeats and Lady Gregory, for, since they adopted it, no doubt has ever arisen as to the belated wisdom of their choice. The theme is one of renunciation, and lends itself to situations of great dramatic intensity, which only so talented an actress as Miss Maire nic Shiubhlaigh could have brought out adequately. Moll Woods, the shuiler, or tramp, singing from door to door, happens upon the cottage of the O'Heas, a childless couple who have adopted a little boy from the neighboring poorhouse. Moll at once recognizes the child as Phil, her son, whom she was obliged to abandon to public charity, and she longs to take him back. But the adopted parents have grown to love the youngster as their own, and are unwilling to part with him. The two women, however, find themselves suddenly united by the arrival of an inspector sent out by the poorhouse authorities to see that the children of the institution are being well cared for by their foster parents. This official is not satisfied with Mrs. O'Hea's care of Phil, and threatens to remove the child. Then the shuiler, sinking her personal feelings, determines to save her son from such a fate.

On her return to the poorhouse she demands admittance, and then claims the child whom she previously deserted. The authorities are legally bound to comply with this request, but once her son is restored to her, Moll Woods takes to the roads again, and comes back to the house of the O'Heas. The latter fear that the child is to accompany his mother in her vagabondage, and endeavor to find employment for Moll, so that even if the boy is torn from them, he will be close at hand and well cared for. At this juncture it transpires that the police have come to arrest the mother for having deserted her child. Then the shuiler's motives are understood; she has formally admitted her relation to the boy in order to claim the sole right to dispose of him. Thereby she saves him from the interference of the authorities, but at the same time places herself within the reach of the law on the old charge of desertion. All her plans for regeneration are ruined, she sacrifices both her own prospects and the possession of her child, in order to insure his future in a good home. As the unfortunate woman stumbles out of the cottage, her hopeless prospects are clear to all who foresee her ultimate release from prison and the drunkenness and vagabondage to which remorse and misery will condemn her. As portrayed by Miss Maire nic Shiubhlaigh, the tragic figure of Moll Woods was one of the most memorable in the history of the Irish Theatre.

The Bribe conforms more nearly to the standard type of "Abbey play", though Seumas O'Kelly has a talent of sufficient strength and individuality to save him from the banalities of the average peasant melodramatist. His subject is the corruptness of domestic politics, a much needed variation from the usual course of dramatizing the political struggle between England and Ireland. Not since the days of the Literary Theatre had there been a serious play dealing with this question, except an unpublished satire of municipal life by Fred Ryan, *The Laying of the Foundation,* which the Fays produced in 1902. As a rule political dishonesty has furnished the material of comedy.

There is no comedy in this somber picture of provincial Ireland, whose central figure is John Kirwan, the chairman of the Garrymore Board of Guardians. It is the duty of this Board to elect a medical officer for the district, and all the usual methods of influencing votes are brought to bear upon the members. Kirwan has resisted them all, even including the discreet offer of a cheque which would be of great help to him, a struggling shopkeeper. Mrs. Kirwan is incensed at his refusal to play the game of politics to his own advantage, and urges various reasons why he should vote for Dr. O'Connor, rather than for Diamond, whom he personally esteems as the better candidate. Kirwan is unmoved by her arguments until he learns that she has borrowed a sum of money which O'Connor's proffered bribe would pay. In a moment of panic he pockets the bribe, and when the Board meets, his deciding vote goes against his old friend Dr. Diamond, who is too poor to buy support. Subsequently he pays for his dishonesty with the life of Mrs. Kirwan and her baby, who are lost through the incompetence of Dr. O'Connor, called in during the illness of the family physician.

The *dénouement* is rather obvious, but it is the only comparatively weak point in the play, which excels in the sober veracity of its uncompromising analysis of provincial manners, political and social. The second act, which takes place in the board-room of the Guardians, is well devised to reveal the sordid vulgarity of those upon whom the welfare of many a community depends. The specific case chosen by Seumas O'Kelly is perhaps the most typical, for such appointments as that of the dispensary doctor are notoriously corrupt in Ireland. Indeed, *The Bribe*, with its interrelation of the numerous influences for evil in our country towns, is a valuable document for all Irishmen. It is, at the same time, a dramatic play, which loses nothing by its careful respect for reality, but rather gains, on comparison with the similar attempts of Lennox Robinson, T. C. Murray, and R. J. Ray.

3

Lord Dunsany

Before examining the work of these representatives of popularity, we must glance at a dramatist of distinction, whom the Abbey Theatre has had the honor

of introducing to the English-speaking world. Next
to his encouragement of Synge, the incident most to
the credit of Yeats's management of the Irish Theatre
was his immediate recognition of Dunsany's dramatic
genius. Prior to 1909, when *The Glittering Gate* was
produced, Dunsany was known to a limited public as
the author of three remarkable works of fantasy,
The Gods of Pegana (1905), *Time and the Gods* (1906),
and *The Sword of Welleran* (1908). In these he set
forth that strange theogony which gave its title to
the first, and whose mythology was elaborated in the
second and third volumes. Instead of seeking his
material in the legendary lore of his country, Dunsany
invented his own myths and legends out of a wealth
of original fancy unique in our time. Not content
with having created a veritable hierarchy of gods to
whom he intrusted the molding of cosmic destinies,
the author made free use of the fabulous Orient which is
the scene of his dramas, and whose description gives
such poetic color to his prose.

Having narrated the adventures of the deities of
Pegana, and interpreted the ceaseless, mysterious
struggle of the world against the onslaught of time
and change, Dunsany was far from exhausting his
imaginative vein. In *A Dreamer's Tales* (1910), *The
Book of Wonder* (1912), and *Fifty-one Tales* (1915),
he has continued to exercise his rare vision of a world
none the less weird because peopled by men rather
than by gods. These collections of short stories and
fables possess all the qualities of the earlier works, but
to the wonder and color of the mythological invention

is added an element of the grotesque and horrible, unsurpassed by Poe and Ambrose Bierce at their best. A certain triviality mars many pages of *Fifty-one Tales*, but the two preceding volumes are almost perfect in their harmonious combination of every element of the fantastic imagination. The superiority of Lord Dunsany is best appreciated when *A Dreamer's Tales* is compared with the stories of Mr. Arthur Machen and Mr. Algernon Blackwood, the only writers of to-day who have tried to exploit the same field.

The plays of Dunsany were collected in 1914 under the commonplace title, *Five Plays*, which included in order of their production *The Glittering Gate*, *King Argimenes*, *The Gods of the Mountain*, *The Golden Doom*, and *The Lost Silk Hat*. Since these were arranged for publication, two others have been produced, *The Tents of the Arabs*, in Paris in 1914, and *A Night at the Inn*, which had its *première* in New York in April, 1915. The text of the latter has not yet been published, but the former appeared in *The Smart Set*, whose editors have done so much to make Dunsany familiar to the American public. All are written out of the author's earlier mood, except *The Glittering Gate* and *The Lost Silk Hat*, which come rather within the scope of his last volume of stories.

When *The Glittering Gate* was produced at the Abbey Theatre in 1909, it was evident that a new force had come into the Dramatic Movement. The little play was simply a dialogue, but so original and unusual in conception that it impressed the audience more than perhaps a substantial drama would have done. Two

burglars, "both dead", stand before the great door of
heaven, and by symbol and conversation the dramatist
expounds their metaphysical beliefs. Their aspirations
are exteriorized in the constantly descending beer
bottles which they eagerly uncork, only to find them
empty. Disappointment spurs them to reflections
upon deity in general, and the failure of the door to
open arouses their professional pride. After careful
examination, they decide to apply their skill, and to
force an entry into paradise. When the gates swing
open, however, the burglars see nothing corresponding to their anticipation of heaven, only stars,
"blooming great stars." With mocking laughter
sounding in their ears, they conclude that such
tricks are typical of malign providence, and that
there is no heaven.

Two years later this curtain-raiser was followed by
Dunsany's second play, *King Argimenes and the Unknown Warrior.* The two acts of *King Argimenes*
gave the true measure of his worth as a dramatist, and
prepared the way for the succeeding dramas of the East.
The enslaved King, Argimenes, is gnawing bones in
the work-fields of King Darniak, together with other
slaves. Their immediate desires are concentrated upon
obtaining a substantial bone to satisfy their hunger.
The opening lines of the play are startling:

King Argimenes   This is a good bone; there is juice
                    in this bone.
Zarb   I wish I were you, Argimenes.
King Argimenes   I am not to be envied any longer. I
                    have eaten up my bone.

But even though hungry, Argimenes is still to be envied for his inner life, filled with memories of former grandeur and domination. He is thus endowed with an advantage over his fellow-slaves which they recognize; he is of the master class. When he finds a sword in the field, and is thereby possessed of the symbol of power, he is impelled to impose his rank. His kingship is accepted by the others, who follow him and overthrow their common oppressor. The finding of the sword acquires the dignity of a miracle, and Argimenes erects a temple to the Unknown Warrior on the spot where his weapon was found.

As effective as the first words of King Argimenes is the closing scene of the play. The death of King Darniak's dog is announced, an animal whose good food had long been a source of envy among the slaves. While sick, he had given rise to much speculation among them as to whether his body would fall to their portion. Greatly they feared lest a lingering death deprive his bones of flesh. Great events have happened since such thoughts troubled the mind of Argimenes, but when the dog dies, the slave memory is still strong:

King Argimenes and his men (savagely and hungrily) Bones!
King Argimenes (remembering what has happened and where he is) Let him be buried with the late King.
Zarb (in voice of protest) Majesty!

Lord Dunsany's longest and best drama is *The Gods of the Mountain*, whose theme is again in the truest vein of the author who invented the theogony of Pegana. Six beggars and a thief impersonate the seven gods of

Marma, "carved out of green jade", who sit upon the mountain top, "with their right elbows resting on their left hand, the right forefinger pointing upwards." The portrayal of these adventurers is perfect in the ease with which their mentality is developed, their cunning aroused, and its effects unrolled before us. Extravagant though it be, the situation convinces the imagination carried away by the excitement of the enterprise, the pose of the beggars in the attitude of the gods, and the gradual belief of the people in the imposture. The pretenders are afraid that the jade deities will be found in their accustomed place, but their uneasiness increases when it is discovered that the green gods have left their site on the mountain. They do not know whether to regard this discovery as a sign of popular credulity, and a proof of their own success. Strange phenomena are witnessed at night, and it is evident that the gods are present. As one man says: "When we see rock walking it is terrible . . . . rock should not walk. When children see it, they do not understand. Rock should not walk in the evening."

Then the beggars are seriously disturbed, but the people have lost all their doubts and believe the gods have come to them. In truth, they have descended upon the city to punish the impostors. It is a wonderful climax when the stone beings enter, point their fingers at the beggars, and petrify them in the traditional attitude of the gods. When the worshippers arrive and find the beggars are really of stone, they are convinced of divinity and reproach themselves with their former skepticism. The irony of this conclusion is delightful, and typical of the whimsical humor of Lord Dunsany. It is significant that his greatest success should have been achieved by the play nearest to his best narrative writing. Compressed to meet the exigencies of the theatre, *The Gods of the Mountain* contains the quintessence of Dunsany.

In *The Golden Doom* the dramatist returned to the one-act form, which is, indeed, sufficient for the rather tenuous subject of the play. A child's rhyme scribbled with a piece of gold on the King's door brings all the prophets and wise men to interpret what they believe to be a message from the gods. Two children wrote the lines innocently while waiting at the door to beg for a hoop, but the soothsayers read into the words the impending doom of their master, who leaves his crown and scepter as an offering to appease the gods. In the evening the children return, and finding a golden hoop and stick, take them in the belief that their prayer for these playthings has been answered. When the King and his advisers observe the disappearance of their sacrificial offerings, they accept the omen as a sign that the gods are pleased, and will stay the doom which was to fall upon them. Thus wisdom and innocence are equally satisfied by an occasion propitious to the exercise of their respective credulities.

The fable is charming, but thoroughly Yeatsian in its lack of specifically dramatic interest. Not so *The Lost Silk Hat*, whose undramatic quality is not compensated by any such delicacy of fancy. It is definitely of that grotesque order which has become more pronounced in Dunsany's latest stories, but whose most powerful expression belongs to an earlier date. The interest centers about the efforts of a gentleman to persuade various persons of humbler rank to retrieve his tall hat from beneath the sofa of a drawing-room where he has just been visiting. His precipitous retreat, we learn, was due to his having quarreled with his hostess, to whom he was engaged to be married. The dialogue alone supports the movement of the play. The Laborer, the Clerk, and the Poet each engage in a discussion as to why they should rescue the hat, and, for reasons most humorously indicated, each refuses. The poet endeavors to fix the gentleman's mind upon the romantic aspect of the situation, and failing that, demands adequate proofs of the reasonableness of fetching the hat. His final disgust, when the gentleman, renouncing romance, enters the house and remains to play a duet on the piano, is equaled only by the emotions of the Laborer when listening to the discourses and arguments of the poet and the owner of the missing article. These characterizations make excellent comedy, though they do not add materially to Lord Dunsany's position as a dramatist.

That his work for the stage is by no means exhausted was made clear by the appearance of the two plays not yet included in his published volume. *The Tents of the Arabs* is an interesting variation upon an ancient theme, and, at the same time, a return to the subject of the mysterious call of the desert, which has inspired so many eloquent pages in Dunsany's stories. The story relates how a King longs for freedom to follow the caravan setting out across the desert to Mecca,

and of his final escape against the wishes of his coun-
sellors. Forgetful of royalty and of the affairs of
state, he lingers a year in the desert, and when the
second act opens we find him on the point of resuming
the slavery of his kingly office. But during his pro-
tracted absence, rumor has it that he has perished, so
that one of the two camel drivers, who were previously
heard regretting the toil of their calling, is emboldened
to claim the throne. His resemblance to the King
helps him, but the servants of state are skeptical, and
demand that Bel-Narb produce some witness of his
claim, other than his fellow conspirator, Aoob. At
this juncture the King, still clothed in the camel-driver's
cloak which he wore in the desert, comes to the impostor's assistance. Seeing a unique opportunity to
obtain permanent liberty, he testifies that Bel-Narb is
in truth the King who departed into the desert twelve
months previously. The latter is received by the
people, and though he offers employment in the palace
to the late King, his proposal is rejected. The King
wants nothing in return for his abdication but freedom
to rejoin the tents of the Arabs.

A Night at the Inn left the impression of being equal
to *The Gods of the Mountain,* which it resembles in
the wonder and horror of its effect. Three sailors, the
survivors of a party which had stolen a great ruby
from the forehead of an Indian god, have been awaiting
some undefined event in a lonely inn for three days
and three nights. The place has been rented by a
dilapidated gentleman to whom they have intrusted
the precious stone. It is his purpose to destroy in this

lonely spot the priests who have dogged the sailors' footsteps since they left India, and have already taken mortal vengeance on the two of their companions in the theft. Sitting with a newspaper in his hand, the gentleman hopes to lure the priests to his attack, so that the sailors may fall upon them and kill them. And so it happens. One by one the three priests enter stealthily, and one by one they are stabbed to death.

The three sailors are delighted at this outcome of their confidence in the gentleman who has so well arranged affairs that they shall enjoy the proceeds of their crime. Drinking and toasting, the four adventurers are celebrating their victory, when their doom comes upon them. Stony footfalls are heard, and soon the guilty men are cowering before the horrible, grotesque jade god, who stamps up to the table, puts the precious ruby in his forehead, and walks out on the lonely moor. Once outside, he calls in dreadful tones to the sailors and their partner to follow him, and as each is named, he is dragged out by some irresistible force. Finally the far-seeing gentleman of fortune obeys the call he had not anticipated, and the inn is occupied only by the bodies of the murdered priests.

Lord Dunsany is the only worthy successor of Yeats in the history of the Irish Theatre up to the present, for he alone has broken with the tradition of peasant drama, and has written plays whose poetry is not concealed by the fact that his medium is prose. For that reason, and because of his mythological and legendary inventiveness, Dunsany seems, to the superficial glance, to be outside the so-called Irish "school", — that popular fiction. He chose Pegana, and the fabulous cities of Babbulkund and Perdondaris, instead of Celtic Ireland and its heroic figures, but his adventures are as stirring to the imagination as any recounted by Gaelic legend. His work, both drama and narrative prose, is part of that rekindling of the flame which has invested the Irish world with the glow of Celtic vision. The marvels he describes are often but the simplest natural phenomena seen through the eyes of a poet, and they take on the glamour and mystery which the Celt has at all times descried in nature. His greatest genius has been revealed in his tales of gods and men, but his contribution to the drama is sufficiently original and important to make the name of a lesser man. The Abbey Theatre is justly proud of its share in making known a writer of so rare a quality. It is such discernment which makes it easy to forget certain sins of omission and commission with which this chapter must close.

4

Melodramatists and Others

Of the host of recruits to the ranks of the "Abbey" playwrights in recent years little need be said. Most of them can write a very creditable melodrama, in which all the peasant formulæ are employed to good effect. Many of the *clichés* of the Boucicault have been abolished, and his situations are frequently reversed, to the great joy of such commentators as Mr.

Bernard Shaw, who imagines that this fact is evidence of lack of old-fashioned patriotism. The process which he recently described as "damning the romantic Old Ireland up hill and down dale" is the modern convention which has replaced the sentimental heroics of an earlier day. Neither is anything more than what the French term *un poncif*, a stereotyped formula, which may or may not correspond to any genuine emotion in the writer. The newer convention finds constant employment at the hands of such playwrights as W. F. Casey, R. J. Ray, T. C. Murray, and Lennox Robinson, whose work is familiar to all who have seen the performances of the Irish Players, at home or abroad. There is nothing reprehensible in the cultivation of native melodrama, and most playgoers will prefer R. J. Ray's *Gombeen Man* to *Arrah na Pogue* or *The Colleen Bawn*. But it is as unnecessary to analyze such work as it is undesirable to give it the prominence which it has latterly obtained in the repertory of the Abbey Theatre.

The poet A. E. described an unpleasantly large number of recent Irish plays when he wrote: "We have developed a new and clever school of Irish dramatists who say they are holding up the mirror to Irish peasant nature, but they reflect nothing but decadence. They delight in the broken lights of insanity, the ruffian who beats his wife, the weakling who is unfortunate in love, and who goes and drinks himself to death." The specific references are clearly to W. F. Casey's *The Man who missed the Tide* and to *The Cross Roads* by Lennox Robinson. Physical suffering, murder, and even pesti-

lence, — among cattle, at least, — are the familiar
expedients by which our playwrights try to escape the
artificial inanities of the successful play of commerce.
By an irony of fate, this violent reaction has merely
resulted in very often substituting these plays with
cheap effects for the restrained and careful work of the
genuine realists.

Lennox Robinson is perhaps the most important of
these writers, for he has shown himself capable of good
work. The plays, however, through which he became
known, are typical illustrations of the melodramatic
tendency. *The Cross Roads* (1909) is merely a series
of violent scenes without much coherence. We are
asked to believe that a woman who marries a man she
does not love brings a curse upon his farm. The tragic
effect of being untrue to oneself is undoubtedly a
theme with dramatic possibilities, but it is too much to
postulate that such a failure should react upon the
fertilizing properties of manure, the laying capacity
of hens, and produce disease among cattle. Yet if
we do not accept this, the play loses all its effect. Instead of sensing the tragedy of the situation, we are
trying to see in the *dénouement* any connection with
what has gone before. The dramatist's next attempt,
while more coherent, was almost as unconvincing.
Harvest (1910) deals with the problem of education as
it affects those whose social condition is not considered
by the authorities when drawing up their plans. The
consequence of training the mind until it is no longer
adapted to its natural environment, while a new outlet
for its activities is lacking, provides in *Harvest* an excuse

for a banal story of seduction, in which the heroine talks the language of old-fashioned melodrama. The characters all are the lifeless mouthpieces of old formulæ, and fail to convey the dramatist's intention.

Strange to say, the first play which Lennox Robinson gave to the Abbey Theatre was better than the two which insured his popularity. *The Clancy Name* (1908), within the short space of one act, contained more humanity than either of its successors. The pride of name in Mrs. Clancy, which made her try to dissuade her son from giving himself up to justice, was a motive which the author was able to develop sympathetically, and which inspired the protagonists with the breath of life. When the youth rushes out to confess his crime to the police, a fine spiritual conflict between the pair has been witnessed, but when we learn that he has been killed while trying to save a child from the hoofs of a runaway horse, we feel that the dramatist has chosen too facile an escape from the dilemma.

His recent plays are concerned with more serious and substantial subjects. *Patriots* (1912) is an interesting picture of the supposedly changed attitude of a younger generation of patriots towards the question of Irish freedom, and the means by which it should be secured. The desertion of the returned political prisoner by men more interested in reformist and Parliamentary methods gave rise to a tragedy whose poignancy is weakened only by the thought that the prestige of Nugent and his insurrectionary faith has been underestimated. The superficiality of the

author's estimate of the psychology of the new generation has now been demonstrated with fearful force.
His own colleagues and contemporaries have been
executed for doing what his play argued was impossible.
Within a week of Lennox Robinson's *début* at the Abbey
Theatre in 1908, *When the Dawn is Come*, by the late
Thomas MacDonagh, was produced. Little more than
a melancholy interest attaches to this unsuccessful
attempt to dramatize an aspect of a situation identical
with that in which MacDonagh was to lose his life.
It is significant, however, that the dramatist who was
to die should have conceived precisely the contrary
circumstances to those depicted by the writer of
Patriots.

Nevertheless the modification of certain political
views is a fact of contemporary Irish life, as witness
the comparatively favorable reception of *The Dreamers*,
which appeared in 1915. Here Lennox Robinson makes
his first attempt at historical drama, by choosing the
final episode in the career of Robert Emmet. Instead,
however, of treating the subject in the traditional ideal-
istic manner, he presents a very depressing account of
the rising and of those who participated in it. Emmet
alone stands out as a man wholly devoted to the cause
of Ireland and prepared to risk everything for success.
His followers are shown to be shiftless, untrustworthy,
and even dishonest, and are made largely responsible
for his failure and death. The play is well constructed
and bears the marks of careful planning and execution,
but it is not easy to accept the author's view of the
causes which led to the collapse of the rebellion. He

is too readily disposed to color the facts in deference to political prejudice. The tolerance extended to this treatment of an almost hallowed subject indicated that lessening of political tension which at one time promised to change the nature of the Irish question. The renewal of just such a tragedy as Emmet's suggests a return to conditions on the point of becoming a memory.

T. C. Murray and R. J. Ray have both contributed to the popular repertory of the Abbey Theatre. The former has published only two plays, *Birthright* (1911) and *Maurice Harte* (1912), neither of which has more than a passing interest. The same is true of *The White Feather* (1909), *The Casting out of Martin Whelan* (1910), and *The Gombeen Man* (1913), by R. J. Ray, none of which has been issued in book form. While T. C. Murray has the same predilection for violent scenes as R. J. Ray, he does not bathe his work in such unrelieved gloom and incredible brutality as distinguish *The White Feather* and *The Gombeen Man*. The last mentioned is a particularly typical example of a theme utterly ruined by bad writing and worse psychology. The drama of this sinister figure in Irish life, the money-lender of the village, is so tangible and moving that only a playwright like Padraic Colum could evoke it. In all its unadorned power he could project the subject into literature, for he alone possesses that sound instinct and knowledge of peasant life which would eliminate the extraneous and unnecessary elements, whose exaggerations are deemed necessary by the imitative realists.

The weakness of the later dramatists is that they are

imitators rather than innovators; they have added nothing to the folk-drama as defined by Synge and Colum, for they have not even emulated Lady Gregory in her folk-history tragedies and comedies. Praise is due to such occasional experimentalists as Norreys Connell, whose one-act play, *The Piper* (1908), and "imaginary conversation," *Time* (1909), were seen for a brief period some years ago. The newcomers whose work has not yet been published show few signs of wishing to contribute something really personal to the repertory of the Irish Theatre, with the exception of A. P. Wilson's study of industrial life, *The Slough* (1914), and perhaps *The Cuckoo's Nest* of John Guinan. But the latter has been followed by *The Plough-Lifters*, a conventional comedy *à la* Boyle, labored and unconvincing. It seems as if the days of peasant realism were nearly over, for the *genre* has become conventionalized to the point of inanition. It is true, Ireland is entitled to have national equivalents for even the worst banalities of the imported English drama. The most commonplace farce or melodrama is rarely quite so futile as its English counterpart, but the Irish Theatre is capable of better things. How it shall continue to realize its original purpose will be suggested when we have concluded our present survey.

CHAPTER VIII

The Ulster Literary Theatre

1

Origins and Environment

PROBABLY because it has had no corporate existence comparable to that of the Abbey Theatre, the Ulster Literary Theatre has escaped the attention of all foreign critics of the Dramatic Revival in Ireland. They have discussed the Ulster playwrights without reference to the circumstances in which the latter have developed, confounding the movement which gave them birth with the numerous amateur organizations, the "Theatre of Ireland", the "Leinster Stage Society", the "National Players", and the "Gaelic Repertory Theatre", whose useful work in fostering Irish drama cannot be overestimated. Nevertheless, the Ulster Theatre is distinguished from all these by reason of its having given birth to a group of writers whose relation to Ulster is more intimate than mere literary association in a given dramatic organization would imply. The regionalism of the Northern dramatists corresponds to a definite condition of Irish geography. One might say that if the Ulster Literary Theatre did not exist, it would be necessary to invent it. The Ulster playwrights are entitled to be considered apart from their Southern contemporaries, even when they have not been identified specifically with the literary movement in Belfast.

The origins of the Ulster Literary Theatre date back to 1902, when the Belfast Protestant National Society decided to widen its hitherto purely political activities by coöperating in the work of the brothers Fay. The latter had just been constituted the successors of the Irish Literary Theatre, and with the assistance of some of their associates, two of the plays, *Cathleen ni Houlihan* and *The Racing Lug* by James Cousins, were produced in Belfast. The effect of this experiment was to strengthen the general determination to give Ulster a share in the Dramatic Revival. After A. E.'s *Deirdre* was performed in Dublin, it was taken to Belfast, and in 1904 the Ulster Literary Theatre came into existence. The inaugural season began in December of that year, when a poetic drama of the heroic age, *Brian of Banba* by Bulmer Hobson, and *The Reformers*, a satire of municipal politics by Lewis Purcell, introduced two new playwrights, both members of the Belfast Protestant National Society.

At the same time the first issue of *Uladh* appeared, containing a manifesto of the Ulster Theatre, and for a short time this review was the Northern counterpart of *Beltaine* and *Samhain*. In its pages, as in those of the latter, were published plays from the repertory of the Theatre, and in the first number appeared *The Little Cowherd of Slainge*, a dramatic legend by Joseph

Campbell, who has since become one of the most notable of the young Irish poets. This little piece, and *The Enthusiast* by Lewis Purcell, were produced the following year, and contributed to the strength of the new enterprise, especial favor being accorded to Purcell's drama of the conflict between Catholic and Protestant, in which a young idealist's failure to reconcile orange and green provided the motive. In 1906 the Ulster Theatre firmly established its claim to serious attention by producing *The Pagan* by Lewis Purcell and *The Turn of the Road* by Rutherford Mayne. These were the first Ulster plays to be issued in permanent form, having been published in 1907.

The Pagan is still the only work of Lewis Purcell available to the reading public. It is a rather curious attempt to extract comedy from the rivalry of Pagan and Christian in sixteenth-century Ireland. A young girl of the new faith is pursued by many suitors, but finally selects a Pagan as the man of her choice, after many diverting scenes. It is a pity that the author has placed no more substantial evidence of his talent on record, but the same is true of the Ulster playwrights in general. Satirical humor, as in this instance, seems to be a dominant characteristic of the Ulster group.

Those who have seen *Thompson in Tir-na-n'Og* and *When the Mist does be on the Bog*, by the writer who signs himself "Gerald MacNamara", — the Ulster dramatists are almost all pseudonymous, — can testify to the intensely comic sense displayed by the author. The choice of the Abbey Theatre for the first production of the last named play gave a piquancy to this good-humored parody of Synge. But none of this work, serious or otherwise, has been published in book form, so that little remains upon which to base an estimate of the Ulster Theatre. Of those associated with that undertaking from the beginning only Rutherford Mayne has collected his work for publication.

Joseph Campbell, it is true, has published one play, as did Lewis Purcell, but *Judgment* (1912) was not written for the Ulster Theatre; it was produced in Dublin by the Irish Players. It is a study of manners among the peasantry of Donegal, and is permeated by that intimate acquaintance with the region which Campbell's prose and poetry had previously revealed.

Those who read his record of a tramp in Donegal, *Mearing Stones* (1911), recognized in the play many echoes of those impressionistic notes of scenes and conversations witnessed while on the road. The action centers about the silent protagonist, Peg Straw, an old and half-demented vagabond, who dominates the situation after the fashion of those invisible forces of Maeterlinckian symbolism. Owen Ban, the weaver, admits to his home the outcast, whom his wife, Nabla, has turned away, but not until the greater part of the first act has passed in conversation relating to this absent figure, who unwittingly gives rise to the movement of the drama. The cries of the poor creature being beaten by other tramps are the signal for her ultimate appearance, for it is then that the weaver disregards his wife's scruples; but Peg crosses his threshold only to die as a result of her injuries. And as this one life is extinguished, another is awakened, when Nabla gives premature birth to a child in consequence of the shock of Peg's death.

In the second act the old woman is laid out for the "wake" which is accorded to even the humblest by Irish peasant custom. The primitive wildness of the death feast is depicted by one familiar with local manners, and gives a tragic horror to the scene, which is increased by the arrival of a wandering stranger, who boisterously disturbs the mourners. In a quarrel he reveals his identity as the son whom popular legend supposed Peg Straw to have killed when he was an infant. Thereupon he is ejected from the house, and denied the privilege of "waking" his dead mother, a summary judgment upon him for his neglect, and a tragedy in the eyes of a peasantry to whom death and the family are the profoundest facts of life.

The technical faults of *Judgment* are so obvious as to require no insistence, yet it is a more valuable addition to the Irish Theatre than most of the relatively well-constructed plays of late years. It is a genuine folk tragedy, deeply rooted in the soil, and characterized by a perfect control of peasant idiom. A sincere sympathy for his people and a deep insight into the manners of the Ulster countryside differentiate Joseph Campbell from those whose sole concern is to adapt the peasant convention to the banalities of superficial melodrama. When he has added a stronger sense of the theatre to his other equipment, he may well rank with the foremost dramatists.

2

The Plays of Rutherford Mayne

It is fortunate that Rutherford Mayne should be the one leader of the Ulster Theatre by whose work we are enabled to measure its significance, for he is not only the best of the Ulster playwrights, but one of the finest talents revealed by the Dramatic Movement. His first play, *The Turn of the Road*, was followed in 1908 by *The Drone*, which was also performed by the Ulster Literary Theatre Society, as almost all this dramatic work has been, with the exception of *The Troth* and one unpublished sketch. In 1912 a collected edition, under the title of *The Drone and other Plays*, brought together his most important writings, *The Turn of the Road*, *The Drone*, *The Troth*, and *Red Turf*. Since then he has written an electioneering farce, *If!*, which was produced at the Abbey Theatre in 1915, but whose publication is doubtful, if one may judge by his failure to reprint his previous essays outside the field of serious folk drama.

The Turn of the Road tells the story of Robbie John Granahan's attempt to stifle the artistic impulse, in obedience to the combined puritanism and practical "good sense" of his friends and relatives. They would rather he married a girl with a good dowry and settle down as a respectable farmer than pursue the fame which his fiddle promises him. He burns his instrument, but cannot forget the prize awarded to him at the *Feis*, or Gaelic musical contest, where his judges promised him a fine career. Granahan is not impelled by the instinct of vagabondage which drove Colum's Conn Hourican on to the roads. A canny Ulsterman, he has a more precisely material advantage to tempt him than the satisfaction of his artistic temperament. Rutherford Mayne has well described the community of well-to-do Protestants, whose opposition to the musician makes such an interesting contrast to the motives at work in *The Fiddler's House*. Although in both plays the artist escapes to fulfill his destiny, all that separates the North of Ireland from the remaining provinces is suggested in the development and atmosphere of the two versions of the same problem.

When *The Drone* was originally played by the Ulster Theatre Society, it was in two acts, but a third act was added when it was revised for publication. Of the purely naturalistic comedies it is supreme in its simple humor and charming portrayal of rural manners. The fun of Lady Gregory's farces seems wholly on the surface when compared with this play, which achieves triumphantly the purpose of William Boyle's *Family Failing*. Daniel Murray has pretended for years that he is working upon an invention which will repay his debt for their continued hospitality. The truth is, this delightful old humbug has never done anything but idle away his days in dreaming. A Scotsman, skeptical as is the wont of his race, demands proofs of Murray's inventiveness, and in spite of the latter's amusing subterfuges, shows him up as an impostor. The drone, however, succeeds eventually in cheating his victims by selling them the bellows which he claims to have invented, and nobody will question the justice of his success, so finely imagined is this character. His charm stands out against the background of harshness and grasping frugality supplied by a typical group of County Down peasants.

Both *The Troth* and *Red Turf* are one-act plays having agrarian crime as their motive. The former describes how Protestant and Catholic unite against their common enemy, the landlord who threatens them with eviction. Ebenezer McKie and Francey Moore determine to shoot Colonel Fotheringham, and pledge themselves that whichever of the two is arrested shall not reveal the identity of his comrade. A shot is heard and McKie returns, his demeanor indicating that the innocent man has been caught by the police. In an agony of fear he waits while his wife watches through the window, and when a neighbor calls to tell of the mad deed of Francey Moore he shrinks from her glance. To Mrs. McKie's question, which is an accusation, he can only reply: "Peace, woman, Moore has no wife." This brief glimpse of another side of the Ulster question is interesting, not only because of its unique place in Mayne's studies of the North Irish peasantry, but also on account of its indication of a fundamental unity between those traditionally depicted as irreconcilable.

The scene of *Red Turf* is Galway, where, of course, every variety of agrarian outrage is deemed natural! But this violent anecdote strains the imagination, even though it takes place on the happy hunting ground of the pseudo-Synge "realists." The murder of one peasant by another, in a quarrel over a bank of turf, is too essentially in the "Abbey" convention to provide serious drama. Strong language and violence, the familiar ingredients, are substituted for thought and action. Yet critics have been found, both here and in Ireland, who profess to regard *Red Turf* as inspired by the study of Synge, though, to do them justice, the Irish comments to this effect have come from the avowed enemies of *The Playboy!*

Rutherford Mayne does not need to write in this manner, as disastrous to his own reputation as to that of the commentators, who have gravely attributed it to the example of Synge. His permanent place in our contemporary dramatic literature has been, and will be, insured by those studies of North Ireland peasant life which he has preserved in the atmosphere and idiom of Ulster. He evokes the subtle characteristics of the one as he has mastered the Biblical rhythms of the other. With the assistance of the Ulster Players, his work has done for the North of Ireland what Synge has done for the West, for the true originality of his achievement is best appreciated in the performances of the Ulster Theatre Society. The setting, speech, and acting combine to impress upon the spectator the peculiar and individual character of the Ulsterman and his environment. Without such affiliations the scope of the Irish Theatre would be incomplete. The work of Rutherford Mayne has, therefore, a general as well as a specific value, for it serves to crystallize the scattered elements of the Dramatic Movement in Ulster, which is fortunate indeed in possessing a representative dramatist of such high quality.

3

St. John G. Ervine

There are no indications that the supremacy of Rutherford Mayne as the leading Ulster playwright will be challenged, in spite of the advent of a newcomer in that field. St. John G. Ervine, though an Ulsterman writing of North Ireland, does not attach himself to the movement which has brought Ulster into the Dramatic Movement. In fact, his participation in the work of the Irish Theatre has been so recent that one cannot regard his work as an integral part of that impulse towards national self-expression in literature and drama, of which the writers heretofore mentioned are the instruments. St. John Ervine did not identify himself with the aspirations and aims of his Irish contemporaries, but preferred to seek in England the opportunities offered by a wider public to talented journalism. It was not until the Irish Plays had become a popular amusement in London and elsewhere that his first play was produced by them. The immediate success of *Mixed Marriage* in 1911 seemed to confirm the wisdom of this retarded entry upon the Irish scene.

Since that date the dramatist has been doubled by the novelist, for, as the author of *Mrs. Martin's Man*, St. John G. Ervine has been greeted with much enthusiasm, and it seemed as if the novel which the Literary Revival has so long awaited had been written. Critical examination of the book, however, soon showed that it was no better than most of the popular fiction

which has had Ireland for its setting in recent years.
The Literary Revival has failed to produce a novelist
comparable to the poets and dramatists to whom
we owe our literary renascence. James Stephens alone
has written prose stories informed by that imaginative
beauty which is the reflection of the Celtic spirit. But
neither *The Crock of Gold* nor *The Demi-Gods* conforms
to the accepted form of the novel, and even *The Char-
woman's Daughter*, for all its apparent conformity to
the rules of the *genre*, is essentially a work of delicate
fantasy.

The superiority of Stephens in the domain of Irish
fiction lies in the intimate relation between his vision
and the genius of the race. *Mrs. Martin's Man* is a
novel, but it is not an *Irish* novel, in any proper sense
of the term. It might have been written by an Englishman, so little does it bear the imprint of the national
spirit. That it was written out of no profound impulse,
but was purely fortuitous in its choice of an Ulster setting, seemed clearly established on the publication of
Alice and a Family. Here the author turned with equal
facility to the lower classes of South London, and produced an amalgam of the sentimental idealizations of
Dickens at his worst and Mr. Pett Ridge at his best.
While some remnants of sincerity marked the external
presentation of the Ulster story, the mechanical composition of humor and pathos marked its successor a deliberate piece of bookmaking.

As a dramatist, St. John G. Ervine owes his reputation to his first play, *Mixed Marriage*, which was published in the Abbey Theatre Series in 1911. Since

that date four other Irish plays by him have been performed: *The Magnanimous Lover, The Critics, The Orangeman*, and *John Ferguson*. All these were issued in a collected edition in 1914, except *John Ferguson*, which was produced and published a year later. They do not represent his complete dramatic works, for he has shown the same versatility in his choice of subject for the theatre as for the novel. *Jane Clegg* (1914), which was played in Manchester and London, is a typical study of middle-class English life, in the manner of Stanley Houghton or D. H. Laurence, showing that the author is not very deeply rooted in his native soil, either as a novelist or a playwright. In fact, until he recently became manager of the Abbey Theatre, nobody suspected him of any desire to be more definitely associated with the intellectual movement of his country than is Mr. Bernard Shaw.

The favorable impression made by *Mixed Marriage* was largely due to the topical nature of the problem presented, and to the justice of the dramatist's treatment of a theme easily susceptible of distortion. The irrepressible conflict of Catholic and Protestant in the North of Ireland had already been dramatized by Lewis Purcell in *The Enthusiast*, but that forgotten one-act play did not grip the popular imagination as did *Mixed Marriage*. St. John Ervine contrived to compress within four acts all the various ramifications of that religious bigotry which has served politicians more usefully than it has served Ulster or Ireland.

John Rainey is described as an Orangeman of at least sufficient intelligence to understand that theological controversy is a poor substitute for coöperation, where the interests of the working classes demand unity. His Protestantism is beyond question, so that he becomes a powerful factor for solidarity, when he urges both Catholic and Protestant to combine in declaring a strike. It looks as if the old trick, by which Belfast capitalism invariably defeats labor, was about to fail. Rainey will prevent the disruption of the forces of the workers by showing them how the employers always raise the religious issue to their own advantage, thus bringing about that paradox of Irish politics: an industrial population devoted to the behests of conservative leaders.

Out of his personal knowledge of social conditions in Belfast, St. John Ervine is able to portray with great veracity the mentality of this Protestant, partly awakened to a sense of actuality. But the latter is soon plunged into the historic past when he discovers that his son, Hugh, intends to marry Nora Murray, a Catholic girl. The red rag of "Popery" is before his eyes, and all his energies are now devoted to stirring up the ancient feud, until the strike is forgotten in a religious riot. The military are called out to quell the rioters, firing is heard in the street before the house, and when Nora rushes out, in helpless protest against this violence, she is shot, thus solving the immediate problem. As for the general question raised by the play, the dramatist has no solution to offer, unless we are to suppose that the intermarriage, which did *not* take place, would have effected the necessary reconciliation of both creeds and the parties which stand for them.

For the English stage an epilogue to this question
was written, and its conclusion is a similar hint of the
regeneration of Ulster which may be expected from the
younger generation. *The Orangeman* was ultimately
included in the Abbey Theatre repertory, after it had
made the round of the English provinces. It tells of
the refusal of young Tom McClurg to carry on the
family tradition of bigotry. His father, a veteran of
the Orange faction, is too old and rheumatic to take
part in the annual demonstration of his co-religionists, in
celebration of the fictitious anniversary of the Battle
of the Boyne. Old McClurg brings out his drum, a
precious heirloom, which he has beaten vigorously every
Twelfth of July, and demands that the son shall take
his place in the parade. Tom McClurg vigorously
repudiates the honor, and clinches his argument by
putting his foot through the drum.

The Magnanimous Lover, the author's second play,
is a rather heavy-handed attempt to expose the moral
prig who presumably lurks in many an Ulster Protestant, as he assuredly does in every puritanical community. Maggie Cather scorns the unctuous remorse
which has prompted her betrayer to offer marriage in
reparation for his fault of ten years ago. Henry Hinde
is an incredible creature, even if he be true to life, and
his fatuous mouthing of Biblical precepts excites neither
humor nor indignation. He is a lifeless target for a
form of satire which only artistic selection could make
interesting. The transcription of a cad's mind is not
itself sufficient to endow the character with any significance. Nor is this weakness compensated by the

changes solemnly rung by Maggie Cather upon the motive of so many feminist dramas : the divine right of woman to bear a child without reference to the legal ceremony of marriage.

Artistic sensitiveness is not the strong point of St. John Ervine, as his characterization of Henry Hinde showed. Not satisfied with this failure to display that power of selection upon which the creative writer has always relied, he proceeded to make bad worse. Spurred by the futile reports in the Irish press of *The Magnanimous Lover,* none of which could ever be dignified by the name of criticism, he wrote a sketch entitled *The Critics.* Bernard Shaw had shown what delightful fun could be had by dramatically criticizing the dramatic critics. This example should have been a warning to his protégé, not an encouragement to ignore his own limitations. In a special note to the printed play, St. John Ervine informs us that the speeches in this wearisome buffoonery are "lifted" from the press notices of *The Magnanimous Lover.* One has no difficulty in believing this, though the fact does little credit to the author's imagination, and adds even less humor to the piece.

A satirical exposure of what passes for criticism in the daily press of most English-speaking countries would be nowhere more effective than in Dublin, but *The Critics* is a reflection upon the reporter who wrote it rather than upon the reporters it vainly essays to satirize. What are we to think of the labored humor which would attribute to even the most ignorant newspapermen the belief that *Hamlet* is an immoral play by an "Ab-

bey" playwright? or that Shakespeare must be the
Gaelic form of the name Murphy? Yet it is with such
obvious fooling that St. John Ervine professes to demon-
strate his superiority to criticism which, in the more
enlightened days of his predecessors, was deservedly
ignored. One would imagine that in failing to appreciate *The Magnanimous Lover*, the commercial press
which vilified Synge and Yeats had finally committed
an outrage upon good taste! A writer who could
include in his collected works such an intellectual
offense as *The Critics*, whose mere performance was
a reflection upon the critical standards of the Irish
Theatre, is obviously disqualified for the task he has
essayed.

On being appointed manager of the Abbey Theatre,
St. John Ervine produced his most recent play, *John
Ferguson* (1915), which had been destined originally
for the English stage. Owing to the precarious state
of the theatre in London during wartime, he decided to
give his work to Dublin, *faute de mieux*, as he was
careful to explain to the reporters. This is his longest
drama since *Mixed Marriage*, both being in four acts,
so that the desire to obtain a more profitable hearing is
easily explained in one whose concern for the Irish
Theatre has been of a rather personal and casual nature.
It must be confessed that, however great its appeal to
a foreign audience, *John Ferguson* is not a very important contribution to the dramatic literature of the Irish
Revival. Like so much that its author has written,
it has secured more praise abroad than at home. An
American critic has been inspired to the point of

declaring it superior in almost every respect to the work of J. M. Synge.

The play is related to *Mixed Marriage* in so far as it is a further illustration of the profound and unrelaxing faith of the religious Ulsterman. John Ferguson is a man of the same caliber as John Rainey in the earlier piece, but his convictions do not work for evil, although powerless to prevent it. His farm is mortgaged to Henry Witherow, the local gombeen-man, in whose power all his friends and neighbors are crushed. The family is waiting anxiously for the remittance from an uncle in America which will save them from eviction and ruin. Ferguson's daughter Hannah tries to conquer her loathing for the mean-spirited James Cæsar, who is willing to marry her and thereby bring the money into the household which would liberate them from Witherow's claims. She thinks she can make the sacrifice, but is obliged to break her promise to Cæsar, who is distracted with grief and shame at being openly scorned by those he would benefit. His feelings are those of madness when he learns that Hannah has been wronged by Witherow, and he swears to carry out a long-standing threat to kill him.

Genuine as his fury is, once Cæsar is on the road to Witherow's house his courage fails him, as it so often did before, and he can only lie in hiding, trembling with rage and fear. While the girl is sobbing at home, "Clutie" John, a local half-wit, goads her brother, Hugh, by his ingenuous talk to such a pitch that he determines to execute the deed which Cæsar failed to accomplish. Unknown to all, he slips out into the night and shoots Witherow, returning unperceived. The wretched man who had openly and so often vowed he would kill the gombeen is of course arrested, and nobody doubts that he is guilty. He even acquires a new dignity on that account in the eyes of Hannah. Her brother eventually confesses, for his principles and those of his father will not permit them to carry out the first impulse to arrange for his escape. Hugh is arrested, and the old father is left to console himself with the comforts of his religion, which has withstood every trial, including, finally, the arrival of the remittance, which would have saved everything by coming one mail sooner.

John Ferguson reverses the natural order of most plays in being summarized, for it gains rather than loses by the process. The obvious banality of certain fundamental incidents does not alter the fact that the motive was soundly dramatic if not particularly new. The central figure, John Ferguson, is an attempt to portray a thoroughly religious, if simple, man, in the presence of disasters sufficient to try the faith of many devout Christians. His creator, however, has failed to infuse real life into him. Misled once again by his naïve confidence in literal transcription, St. John Ervine conceives of no more effective means of characterizing John Ferguson than that of making him constantly read aloud, or repeat, long texts of Scripture. These lay sermons are excessive, and overshoot the mark. Similarly, in order that we may know James Cæsar for a coward, the author makes of him a monstrous caricature, who utters openly all the craven thoughts of the meanest-spirited creature conceivable to the average man. Both these characters remind one of those symbolical personages in the medieval allegories, whose significance was writ large upon them in the most primitive fashion, so that there should be no mistake as to their identity.

This crude characterization by means of externals, this purely mental conception of human types, reveals St. John Ervine as in the category of the melodramatists. He does not write out of any vision; he does not speak with the authentic voice of one whose impulse comes straight from the life and spirit of his own people. Excepting John Rainey in *Mixed Marriage*, there is not a character in these plays who is more than a mere verbal statement of a point of view, a labeled puppet through whom the author tries to convey his intentions. Speeches are no more a substitute for characterization than words are for drama, unless perhaps where a Bernard Shaw is concerned. He alone has made the exposition of ideas a satisfactory alternative to the portrayal of life. St. John Ervine has not the intellectual power of formulating ideas in such a manner as to visualize a whole class and a philosophy. He has not that faculty which can evoke the mentality of a nation as in Broadbent of *John Bull's other Island*. The Ulster dramatist would believe himself to have done so, if he had put into Broadbent's mouth faithful and frequent quotations from the English Liberal newspapers! By their words only, he seems to say, you shall know them.

If John Ferguson and Henry Hinde do not convince us as being more than mechanical representations of

preconceived types, that is because they are not born
of sympathetic insight and observation, but are
attempts to reproduce verbally the author's recollections of what such people say. They speak before us,
but do not live before us. In almost all that St. John
Ervine has written for the stage, reporting does duty
for the creation and development of character. In
his novels, whatever there is of reality is due to the
same methods, but, in the main, he relies upon the
elaboration of literary conventions, notably where
women are concerned. Mrs. Martin and Alice are the
stock figures of sentimental feminism. On the one
hand is the martyred and indomitable wife, who, sur-
viving her husband's worst offenses, manages to keep
everything respectable; on the other, the familiar
child of "mothering" proclivities, who triumphs by
innocence and precocious wisdom in a world of corrupt and incompetent adults. The author of *Alice
and a Family* has not studied life; he has studied
Dickens, making a special note of "Little Dorrit" and
"The Marchioness." The women of both the plays and
the novels are, in short, prolonged statements of "what
every woman knows"; solemn demonstrations of the
amiable platitude: "the hand that rocks the cradle
rules the world."

It is not within the province of the present work to
estimate the position of St. John Ervine in contemporary English Literature. It may well be that his reputation in England is assured, for it is to that public he
originally addressed himself, his connection with the
Irish Theatre, and his interest in Ireland, being, as it

were, an afterthought. It is certain that appreciation
abroad will atone for the rather anomalous nature of his
sudden relationship to a national movement with which
he has, as an artist, little in common. A leading review
in this country recently stated that "Synge at his best is
superior to Mr. Ervine in sheer imaginative power, but
a large part of his work is tainted with a kind of insanity, and he has nothing like Mr. Ervine's firm grasp of
reality." That criticism is typical of the attitude of
the press, outside Ireland, towards the author of *Mrs.
Martin's Man*, his first popular success, which was
vouched for by that expert in nationality, Mr. H. G.
Wells. Bernard Shaw describes him as "a genuine
Irishman of genius", the inference being that those
writers who have lived and worked in Ireland all their
lives, and have felt the urge of the national spirit in
literature, are not genuine.

These encomiums, however justified, can have little
bearing upon the question which falls within our present
scope. We must determine the value of St. John Ervine's work as part of the dramatic literature which
owes its impulse to the forces that have built up the
Irish Theatre. We have seen the character of the
drama inspired by the traditions and ideals of a movement which has been a veritable literary renaissance in
Ireland. How far does *John Ferguson* or *Mixed Marriage* correspond to the standards and purpose of the
Dramatic Revival? It would seem as if neither had
contributed materially to the realization of those aims
which were before the pioneers and collaborators in
the enterprise whose history has been outlined. St.

John Ervine belongs definitely to the new régime, which was forecasted by the gradual elimination of all but the more popular plays and playwrights from the current repertory of the Abbey Theatre. It is fitting and significant that he should now be manager of an institution with which he was not associated until the process of change was under way.

His plays are not Irish in the sense that those of his predecessors were; they are not the expression of any profound or essential phase of our national life and being. They have neither the poetic, imaginative quality of Yeats or Synge, nor do they bear the imprint of the folk spirit which is the possession of Padraic Colum and the genuine peasant dramatists. Whatever their respective merits and demerits, all the writers heretofore mentioned have endeavored, with varying success, it is true, to dramatize those elements of our civilization which are fundamentally and specifically Irish. Some have felt the poetry, others the tragedy; some have seen only the humor, others the superficial drama, of Ireland — but, with negligible exceptions, none have written in a mood indifferent, or alien, to the spirit of the race.

St. John Ervine must be counted amongst those exceptions. He has not divined any vital situation arising out of the character of the Irish people and the composition of Irish society. His presentation of the political conflict in Ulster, a relatively superficial and transitory condition, is the only instance where he has given dramatic expression to a genuine Irish problem. The other plays produced at the Abbey Theatre had no more claim to the national stage than *Jane Clegg*, which is frankly English in its conception and appeal. Remove the Ulster accent from *The Magnanimous Lover* and *John Ferguson*, and there is no reason why they also should not be dedicated to Shaw, and addressed directly to the same audience. In fine, this dramatist is at bottom a journalist, with an eye for the external peculiarities of Irish life; hence *Mixed Marriage*.

That he is a good journalistic commentator on Irish political and social issues is proved by his entertaining study, *Sir Edward Carson and the Ulster Movement* (1915), where the hollowness of the question treated in *Mixed Marriage* is demonstrated with great skill. Such comment is open to all Irishmen, however expatriate, provided they stimulate intelligent discussion, and St. John Ervine has established his right in this field more effectively than in the domain of Anglo-Irish literature. So far as the latter is concerned, he seems destined to be another of those Irishmen, like Wilde and Shaw (to name the inevitable pair), whose fame can never be identified with any other country but that of their literary naturalization.

CHAPTER IX

Now that the Irish Theatre has entered upon a new phase of its existence, it is possible to sum up its present achievement. All the circumstances of the past few years indicate that a chapter in its history has closed, and that, whatever the future may bring, there can be no return to the conditions which prevailed until the death of Synge in 1909. It is not likely that the Abbey Theatre will disappear, for it has overcome difficulties which often threatened to make survival a miracle. Neither the European war, nor the devastation of Dublin during the insurrection of April, 1916, has destroyed it. Early in 1915 disquieting reports hinted at the abandonment of the enterprise, but W. B. Yeats was able to affirm his intention of weathering the world-storm. As if to confirm the hope of permanence, the Theatre itself survived intact the destruction of all the neighboring buildings when the Irish capital was besieged.

What has been said of the late dramatists should make it easy to understand why a change in the program of the National Theatre has become imperative. So long as the folk drama and the poetic drama of Irish legend were encouraged, there was a certain

193

homogeneity of purpose and spirit, but the complacent substitution of melodrama and farce made for disintegration. Intelligent playgoers could not be found to tolerate the eternal repetitions of the popular playwrights, who did not even promise them the humor of peasant speech which distinguishes Lady Gregory's writings from the others. Consequently, the quality of both the plays and their audiences underwent a subtle change, until finally nothing remained of the original tradition but an occasional performance of Yeats and Synge. Even when the Irish Players went on tour they began to meet with the same complaints as had deprived them of their best supporters in Ireland. Moreover the Players themselves were no longer the same; they had lost too many of their best actors, the brothers Fay, Miss Sara Allgood, Miss Moira O'Neill, Miss Maire nic Shiubhlaigh and Miss Eithne Magee. The newcomers, players and playwrights alike, were living on the achievements of their predecessors.

Just as this process of deterioration had reached its height, Edward Martyn found circumstances favorable to the resuscitation of his early plans. "The Irish Theatre" was launched in 1914, to carry on the work of the Irish Literary Theatre and the various amateur theatrical associations which had been inspired by that example. All these scattered energies had been devoted to the support of the drama which did not come within the scope of the National Theatre. Reference has already been made to the success of this experiment, in which Martyn had the assistance of the late Thomas

MacDonagh and Joseph Plunkett. It is to be feared that the tragic termination of the career of these writers, and the imprisonment of others who had collaborated with Martyn and MacDonagh, may have the effect of killing the Irish Theatre in embryo. The only alternative would be a junction of forces between the Abbey Theatre and the other organization. In other words, that divergence of aims which at the outset dissolved the partnership of Martyn and Yeats must be compromised.

There is no reason why *The Heather Field, The Shadowy Waters, The Playboy of the Western World,* and *The Land* should not be part of the same repertory. It is no less narrow to restrict the programs of the National Theatre to psychological than to peasant plays, and both branches of the Dramatic Movement have suffered by this dissociation. While Martyn's program had to be resigned to amateurs, Yeats's has been seriously threatened by the exigencies of commercial success. Similarly, the Ulster Literary Theatre Society purchased its independence at the cost of its corporate existence. Instead of becoming an integral part of the Abbey Theatre, the Ulster Theatre condemned itself to a precarious and intermittent career, producing its plays anywhere and everywhere, in competition with the playhouses of commerce. Occasional visits to the National Theatre in Dublin were the only signs of the original affiliation, and almost all the Ulster plays have had their first nights in Belfast. Until Rutherford Mayne's *If!* was produced last year, none had its *première* at the Abbey Theatre.

Should St. John Ervine carry out the avowed intention of his management, we may expect the Irish Theatre to become, not a national institution, but a provincial English repertory theatre. Himself a dramatist in the English, rather than the Irish, tradition, he will have no difficulty in effecting such a change. In fact he has publicly indicated the nature of his proposed innovations by promising the production of Milton's *Samson Agonistes* and Beaumont and Fletcher's *The Knight of the Burning Pestle.* Coupled with his constant assurances of the non-existence of good Irish plays, such announcements suggest the advent of a subsidiary branch of the London Court Theatre or Stage Society. Nobody familiar with the dramatic literature of the Irish Revival would have much difficulty in proposing works of more national interest to replace these, and to rid their sponsor of his illusion that the native drama is an exhausted vein. With a little more sympathy for the achievement of his predecessors, he would have an unusual opportunity to bring about that union of forces which is desirable. The whole field of Irish drama might be represented, at last, by the repertory of the Abbey Theatre. Once that had been accomplished, the production of foreign masterpieces, whether by Milton or Hauptmann, would be welcomed by all educated Irishmen. As it is, both Edward Martyn and Lady Gregory have been instrumental in making known much of the best work of the Continental dramatists, ancient and modern.

Such a compromise, if it be correct to use that term, would not only be to the advantage of our dramatic literature; it would save the National Theatre from the worse compromise of abandoning its finest ideals. There is little use in saving its nominal life at the expense of its artistic soul. If it ceases to stand for those ideals so eloquently formulated by Yeats in the pages of *Samhain*, and so well defended and exemplified in the first decade of the Theatre's history, the loss will be hard for Ireland to replace. No satisfaction would then be derived from the thought that the Abbey Theatre was doing good service to the general repertory movement in England. If the Literary Revival has meant a great deal to us, the reason must be sought in the fact that it was always something more than "mere literature." It has been a manifestation of nationality, which has given us a literature and a theatre essentially different from those of any other English-speaking country.

After long years of purely political struggle, the soul of Ireland once more found expression in literature. When Gaelic ceased to be the medium of education, those who found themselves obliged to use English were cut off from contact with national culture, and could only attach themselves to the traditions of the new tongue. Then came the period of the anglicized Irish writers, — Goldsmith, Swift, and the others. The contrast between the poetry of the eighteenth century and that of the last fifty years gives the exact measure of the importance of the Celtic renaissance: W. B. Yeats cannot be mistaken for an English poet. Similarly, Synge is an Irish dramatist in a sense which makes the adjective meaningless when applied to Sher-

idan or Oscar Wilde. The mere accident of birth in
Ireland has never been sufficient to entitle a writer to a
place beside those who have given us a national literature.

In an early number of *Samhain*, Yeats rejected, by
implication, many who have since been admitted to
the Irish Theatre, when he said : " If our organizations
were satisfied to interpret a writer to his own countrymen merely because he was of Irish birth, the organizations would become a kind of trade-union for the help-
ing of Irishmen to catch the ear of London publishers
and managers, and for upholding writers who had been
beaten by abler Englishmen." In view of contemporary circumstances that passage sounds prophetic.
"Let a man turn his face to us," wrote Yeats in 1904,
"accepting the commercial disadvantages that would
bring upon him, and talk of what is near our hearts,
Irish Kings and Irish Legends and Irish Countrymen, we
would find it a joy to interpret him." We have, however, changed all that under the later régime. The
Abbey Theatre is now at the disposal of rising and accepted London playwrights, whenever their usual mar-
ket is not available, and it will tend to be so increasingly, unless some halt is called.

Nevertheless, looking over the first ten years of the
Irish National Theatre, one cannot but be impressed by
the high quality of its achievement. What Yeats
asked for at the outset has been granted ; "the half-
dozen minds who are likely to be the dramatic imagination of Ireland for this generation" have produced their
work, and secured an audience. In addition to the

dramatists of the first importance, there are the others, who have been adversely criticized, not so much because of their inferior workmanship as on account of their prominence in the programs of the Abbey Theatre. It would be absurd to pretend, or expect, that every playwright must be of the same merit. There is room for farce and melodrama, of the most elementary kind, provided they be assigned to their proper place. Even the worst have not yet reached the depths of the same class of play in the theatre of commerce, and are, therefore, preferable.

The Irish Theatre does not address itself to a clique only, but to the general public, and it must undoubtedly cater for many tastes. Let us hope that it will continue to do so, always remembering and enforcing those standards and ideals which were its point of departure and its greatest strength. It would be a pity if its destinies should be intrusted to those who were ignorant, or contemptuous, of the traditions which have given dramatists to Ireland worthy of her poets. It is to the encouragement of such dramatists that everything must be subordinated, if the National Theatre is to justify its name, and prove equal to the task so courageously and successfully initiated sixteen years ago.

BIBLIOGRAPHICAL APPENDIX

I

CONTEMPORARY IRISH DRAMATISTS

The dates on the left are those of the first performance. On the right are the date and place of *first* publication in book form, unless when otherwise indicated.

A. E. (GEORGE W. RUSSELL).

    1902.   Deirdre. Dublin, 1907.
              Republished in "Imaginations and Reveries."
                 Dublin, 1915; New York, 1916.

BOYLE, WILLIAM.

    1905.   The Building Fund. Dublin, 1905.
    1906.   The Eloquent Dempsey. Dublin, 1907.
    1906.   The Mineral Workers. Dublin, 1907.
    1912.   Family Failing. Dublin, 1913.

CAMPBELL, JOSEPH.

    1905.   The Little Cowherd of Slainge: in "Uladh",
              November, 1904.
    1912.   Judgment. Dublin, 1912.
              The Turn-out: in "The Irish Review", August, 1912.

COLUM, PADRAIC.

    1903.   The Saxon Shilling.
    1903.   Broken Soil, revised as The Fiddler's House.

1905. The Land. Dublin, 1905.

1907. The Fiddler's House. Dublin, 1907.

1908. The Miracle of the Corn: in "Studies." Dublin, 1907.

1910. Thomas Muskerry. Dublin, 1910.

1910. The Destruction of the Hostel: in "A Boy in Eirinn." New York, 1913; London, 1916.

The Desert. Dublin, 1912. Under title "Mogu the Wanderer." Boston, 1917.

1913. The Betrayal.

DUNSANY, LORD.

1909. The Glittering Gate.

1911. King Argimenes and the Unknown Warrior.

1912. The Golden Doom.

1913. The Lost Silk Hat.

All in "Five Plays." London and New York, 1914.

1914. The Tents of the Arabs: in "The Smart Set", March, 1915.

1915. A Night at an Inn.

ERVINE, ST. JOHN G.

1911. Mixed Marriage. Dublin, 1911.

1912. The Magnanimous Lover. Dublin, 1912.

1913. The Critics.

1913. The Orangeman.

All in "Four Plays." Dublin, 1914.

1913. Jane Clegg. London, 1914; New York, 1915.

1915. John Ferguson. Dublin, 1915; New York, 1916.

FITZMAURICE, GEORGE.

1907. The Country Dressmaker. Dublin, 1914.

1908. The Pie-dish.

1913. The Magic Glasses.

The Moonlighter.

The Dandy Dolls.

    All in "Five Plays." Dublin, 1914; Boston, 1917.

GREGORY, LADY.

1904. Spreading the News: in "Spreading the News and other Comedies." Dublin, 1907.

1905. Kincora. Dublin, 1905.

1905. The White Cockade. Dublin, 1905.

1906. Hyacinth Halvey: in "Seven Short Plays." Dublin and Boston, 1909.

1906. The Gaol Gate: in "Seven Short Plays."

1906. The Canavans: in "Irish Folk-History Plays." London and New York, 1912.

1907. The Jackdaw: in "Seven Short Plays."

1907. The Rising of the Moon: in "Spreading the News and other Comedies."

1907. The Poorhouse: in "Spreading the News and other Comedies."

1907. Devorgilla: in "Irish Folk-History Plays."

1907. The Unicorn from the Stars (in collaboration with W. B. Yeats). New York, 1908.

1908. The Workhouse Ward: in "Seven Short Plays."

1909. The Image. Dublin and Boston, 1910.

1910. The Travelling Man: in "Seven Short Plays."

1910. The Full Moon: in "New Comedies." London and New York, 1913.

1910. Coats: in "New Comedies."

1911. The Deliverer: in "Irish Folk-History Plays."

1912. MacDarragh's Wife, revised as McDonough's Wife: in "New Comedies."

1912. The Bogie Men: in "New Comedies."

1912. Damer's Gold: in "New Comedies."

Grania: in "Irish Folk-History Plays."

1915. Shanwalla.

The Golden Apple. London, 1916.

MACDONAGH, THOMAS.

1908. When the Dawn is Come. Dublin, 1908.

1908. Sweet Innisfail.

1912. Metempsychosis: in "The Irish Review", February, 1912.

1915. Pagans.

MARTYN, EDWARD.

1899. The Heather Field. London, 1899.

1900. Maeve. London, 1899.

1904. An Enchanted Sea. London, 1902.

1905. The Tale of a Town. London, 1902.

1912. Grangecolman. Dublin, 1912.

1914. The Dream Physician.

1915. The Privilege of Place.

MAYNE, RUTHERFORD.

1906. The Turn of the Road. Dublin, 1907; Boston, 1917.

1908. The Drone. Dublin, 1909; Boston, 1917.

1908. The Troth. Dublin, 1909; Boston, 1917.

1909. The Gomeril.

1910. The Captain of the Hosts.

1911. Red Turf: in "The Drone and other Plays." Dublin, 1912; Boston, 1917.

1915. If!

MOORE, GEORGE.

1900. The Bending of the Bough. London and Chicago, 1900.

1901. Diarmuid and Grania (in collaboration with W. B. Yeats).

MURRAY, T. C.
    1909. The Wheel of Fortune.
    1910. Birthright. Dublin, 1911.
    1912. Maurice Harte. Dublin, 1912.

O'KELLY, SEUMAS.
    1907. The Matchmakers. Dublin, 1908.
    1908. The Flame on the Hearth : in " Three Plays."
          Dublin, 1912.
    1909. The Shuiler's Child. Dublin, 1909.
    1910. The Homecoming : in " Three Plays."
    1914. The Bribe. Dublin, 1914.

PURCELL, LEWIS.
    1904. The Reformers.
    1905. The Enthusiast.
    1906. The Pagan. Dublin, 1907.

ROBINSON, LENNOX.
    1908. The Clancy Name : in "Two Plays." Dublin,
          1911.
    1909. The Cross Roads. Dublin, 1911.
    1909. The Lesson of Life.
    1910. Harvest : in "Two Plays."
    1912. Patriots. Dublin, 1912.
    1915. The Dreamers. Dublin, 1915.

SYNGE, JOHN M.
    1903. In the Shadow of the Glen. London, 1905.
    1904. Riders to the Sea. London, 1905.
    1905. The Well of the Saints. Dublin, London, 1905.
    1907. The Playboy of the Western World. Dublin,
          1907.
    1909. The Tinker's Wedding. Dublin, 1907.
    1910. Deirdre of the Sorrows. Dublin, 1910.
          All in Collected Works. Dublin, 1910;
          Boston, 1911.

YEATS, WILLIAM BUTLER.

1894. The Land of Heart's Desire. London and Chicago, 1894.

1899. The Countess Cathleen. London and Boston, 1892.

1901. Diarmuid and Grania.

1902. Cathleen ni Houlihan. London, 1902.

1902. The Pot of Broth: in "Plays for an Irish Theatre", vol. II. London and New York, 1904.

1903. The Hour Glass. London, 1903.

1903. The King's Threshold: in "Plays for an Irish Theatre", vol. III. London, 1904.

1904. The Shadowy Waters. London, 1900; New York, 1901.

1904. On Baile's Strand: in "Seven Woods." Dundrum and New York, 1903.

1904. Where there is Nothing. London and New York, 1903.

1906. Deirdre. London, 1907.

1907. The Unicorn from the Stars (in collaboration with Lady Gregory). New York, 1908.

1908. The Golden Helmet. New York and Stratford-on-Avon, 1908.

1910. The Green Helmet. Dundrum and New York, 1910.

1916. The Player Queen.

See also Poetical Works: Volume II, Dramatical Poems, New York, 1907; Collected Works in Verse and Prose, 8 volumes, Stratford-on-Avon, 1908; and subsequent collected editions.

II

CRITICAL WORKS

ANDREWS, CHARLTON. The Drama To-day. Philadelphia, 1913.

ARCHER, WILLIAM. Poets of the Younger Generation. London, 1902.

BICKLEY, FRANCIS. J. M. Synge and the Irish Dramatic Movement. London and Boston, 1912.

BITHELL, JETHRO. W. B. Yeats. Paris, 1913.

BORSA, MARIO. *Il Teatro Inglese Contemporaneo.* Milan, 1906; London and New York, 1908.

BOURGEOIS, MAURICE. J. M. Synge and the Irish Theatre. London, 1913.

BOYD, ERNEST A. Ireland's Literary Renaissance. New York, 1916.

BROWN, STEPHEN J. A Guide to Books on Ireland, Part I. Dublin, 1912.

CARTER, HUNTLY. The New Spirit in Drama and Art. London, 1912.

CHANDLER, F. W. Aspects of Modern Drama. New York, 1914.

CLARK, B. H. British and American Drama of To-day. New York, 1915.

ELTON, OLIVER. Modern Studies. London, 1907.

FIGGIS, DARRELL. Studies and Appreciations. London and New York, 1912.

GREGORY, LADY AUGUSTA. Our Irish Theatre. New York, 1913; London, 1914.

GWYNNE, STEPHEN. To-Day and To-Morrow in Ireland. Dublin, 1903.

HAMILTON, CLAYTON. Studies in Stagecraft. New York, 1915.

HONE, J. M.　W. B. Yeats.　Dublin, 1915; New York, 1916.

HOWE, P. P.　The Repertory Theatre.　London, 1910.
J. M. Synge.　A Critical Study.　London and New York, 1912.

HUNEKER, JAMES.　The Pathos of Distance.　New York and London, 1913.

JACKSON, HOLBROOK.　All Manner of Folk.　London and New York, 1912.
The Eighteen Nineties.　London and New York, 1913.

KENNEDY, J. M.　English Literature: 1880–1905.　London, 1912.

KRANS, H. S.　W. B. Yeats and the Irish Literary Revival.　New York, 1904; London, 1905.

LEWISOHN, L.　The Modern Drama.　New York, 1915.

MAIR, G. H.　English Literature: Modern.　London and New York, 1911.
Modern English Literature.　London and New York, 1914.

MALYE, JEAN.　La Littérature Irlandaise Contemporaine.　Paris, 1913.

MASEFIELD, JOHN.　John M. Synge: A Few Personal Recollections.　Dundrum and New York.　1915.

MASON, EUGENE.　A Book of Preferences in Literature.　London, 1915; New York, 1916.

MONAHAN, M.　Nova Hibernia.　New York, 1914.

MONTAGUE, C. E.　Dramatic Values.　London and New York, 1911.

MOORE, GEORGE.　Hail and Farewell.　3 vols.　London and New York, 1911–1914.

NEVINSON, H. W.　Books and Personalities.　London and New York, 1905.

OLIVER, D. E. The English Stage: Its Origins and
Modern Development. London, 1912.

OLIVERO, F. *Studi sul Romanticismo Inglese.* Bari, 1914.

PAUL-DUBOIS, L. *L'Irlande Contemporaine.* Paris, 1907;
Dublin, 1911.

REID, FORREST. W. B. Yeats; A Critical Study. London and New York, 1915.

WALBROOK, H. M. Nights at the Play. London, 1911.

WALKLEY, A. B. Drama and Life. London, 1907; New
York, 1911.

WEYGANDT, C. Irish Plays and Playwrights. Boston
and London, 1913.

YEATS, W. B. The Cutting of an Agate. New York,
1912.

III

PERIODICALS

BEWLEY, CHARLES. The Irish National Theatre. Dublin Review, January, 1913.

BICKLEY, FRANCIS. Deirdre. Irish Review, July, 1912.

BIRMINGHAM, GEORGE. The Literary Movement in Ireland. Fortnightly Review, December, 1907.

BOURGEOIS, MAURICE. Synge and Loti. Westminster
Review, May, 1913.

BOYD, ERNEST A. The Abbey Theatre. Irish Review,
February, 1913.
    Le Théâtre Irlandais. Revue de Paris, September 1,
1913.

CAZAMIAN, MADELEINE. *Le Théâtre de J. M. Synge.
Revue du Mois,* October, 1911.

CLARK, JAMES M. The Irish Literary Movement. *Eng-
lische Studien,* July, 1915.

210 THE CONTEMPORARY DRAMA OF IRELAND

COLUM, PADRAIC. The Irish Literary Movement.
Forum, January, 1915.

CONNELL, NORREYS. John Millington Synge. English
Review, June, 1909.

DUNCAN, E. M. The Writings of W. B. Yeats. Fortnightly Review, February, 1909.

DUNSANY, LORD. Romance and the Modern Stage.
National Review, July, 1911.

GUNNELL, DORIS. *Le Nouveau Théâtre Irlandais. La
Revue*, January 1, 1912.

GUNNING, G. HAMILTON. The Decline of the Abbey
Theatre Drama. Irish Review, February, 1912.

GWYNNE, STEPHEN. The Irish Theatre. Fortnightly
Review, 1901.
  The Uncommercial Theatre. Fortnightly Review,
December, 1902.

MACGRATH, JOHN. W. B. Yeats and Ireland. Westminster Review, July, 1911.

MAGUIRE, MARY C. John Synge. Irish Review, March,
1911.

MENCKEN, H. L. Synge and Others. Smart Set, October, 1912.

MENNLOCH, WALTER. Dramatic Values. Irish Review,
September, 1911.

MONTGOMERY, K. L. Some Writers of the Celtic Renaissance. Fortnightly Review, September, 1911.

REID, FORREST. The Early Work of W. B. Yeats. Irish
Review, January, 1912.

TENNYSON, CHARLES. Irish Plays and Playwrights.
Quarterly Review. July, 1911.
  The Rise of the Irish Theatre. Contemporary Re-
view, August, 1911.

INDEX

211

Fay's Irish National Dramatic Company, 33, 34, 36, 39, 64, 71, 111, 122, 140
Feast of Bricriu, The, 83
Ferguson, Samuel, 48
Fiddler's House, The (*Broken Soil*), 119, 176
  Discussed, 112–113
  Published, 112
Fifty-one Tales, 154–155
Fitzmaurice, George, 143–149
  Rank of, 149
  Use of idiom, 145, 147, 148–149
  Works: *Country Dressmaker, The*, 143, 144–145, 146, 147
    Dandy Dolls, The, 144, 147–148
    Magic Glasses, The, 144, 147–148
    Moonlighter, The, 144, 146–147
    Pie-dish, The, 143, 144, 145–146
Five Plays (Dunsany), 155
Five Plays (Fitzmaurice), 144, 145
Foleys, The, 111
Fool of the World, The, 74
Freie Bühne (Theatre), 1
Full Moon, The, 128, 129

Gaelic drama, 4
  Literature, 4
Gaelic Repertory Theatre, 170
Gaiety Theatre, Manchester, 39
Gaol Gate, The, 127, 128, 137
General John Regan, 129, 130
Ghosts, 17, 112
Giraldi, Giovanni, 4

Glittering Gate, The, discussed, 155–156
  Produced, 154, 155
  Published, 155
Gods and Fighting Men, 123
Gods of Pegana, The, 154
Gods of the Mountain, The, 161
  Discussed, 157–159
  Published, 155
Golden Doom, The, discussed, 159
  Published, 155
Goldsmith, Oliver, 197
Gombeen Man, The, 164, 168
Gonne, Miss Maud, 66
Grangecolman, discussed, 28–29
  Produced, 28
Grania, 130, 136
  Discussed, 132–134
Green Helmet, The (*Golden Helmet*), 52, 134
  Discussed, 83–84
  Produced, 83
Gregory, Lady, 6, 34, 36, 37, 39, 64, 71, 83, 104, 121, 143, 149, 150, 176, 194, 196
  Collaboration with Yeats, 64, 67, 70, 71, 72, 122–123
  Comedies, 126–130
  Debt to O'Grady, 124
  Folk history plays, 130–138
  Kiltartan English, 105, 126
  Literary position, 123, 138
  Miscellaneous works: *Book of Saints and Wonders, A*, 123, 125
    Cuchulain of Muirthemne, 83, 105, 123, 124–125
    Gods and Fighting Men, 123